Contemporary Debates in Holocaust Education

DOI: 10.1057/9781137388575.0001

Other Palgrave Pivot titles

Teresa A. Fisher: Post-Show Discussions in New Play Development

Judith Baxter: Double-Voicing at Work: Power, Gender and Linguistic Expertise

Majid Yar: Crime, Deviance and Doping: Fallen Sports Stars, Autobiography and the Management of Stigma

Grace Ji-Sun Kim and Jenny Daggers: Reimagining with Christian Doctrines: Responding to Global Gender Injustices

L. H. Whelchel, Jr.: Sherman's March and the Emergence of the Independent Black Church Movement: From Atlanta to the Sea to Emancipation

G. Douglas Atkins: Swift, Joyce, and the Flight from Home: Quests of Transcendence and the Sin of Separation

David Beer: Punk Sociology

Owen Anderson: Reason and Faith in the Theology of Charles Hodge: American Common Sense Realism

Jenny Ruth Ritchie and Mere Skerrett: Early Childhood Education in Aotearoa New Zealand: History, Pedagogy, and Liberation

Pasquale Ferrara: Global Religions and International Relations: A Diplomatic Perspective

François Bouchetoux: Writing Anthropology: A Call for Uninhibited Methods

Robin M. Lauermann: Constituent Perceptions of Political Representation: How Citizens Evaluate their Representatives

Erik Eriksen: The Normativity of the European Union

Jeffery Burds: Holocaust in Rovno: A Massacre in Ukraine, November 1941

Timothy Messer-Kruse: Tycoons, Scorchers, and Outlaws: The Class War That Shaped American Auto Racing

Ofelia García and Li Wei: Translanguaging: Language, Bilingualism and Education

Øyvind Eggen and Kjell Roland: Western Aid at a Crossroads: The End of Paternalism

Roberto Roccu: The Political Economy of the Egyptian Revolution: Mubarak, Economic Reforms and Failed Hegemony

Stephanie Stone Horton: Affective Disorder and the Writing Life: The Melancholic Muse

Barry Stocker: Kierkegaard on Politics

Michael J. Osborne: Multiple Interest Rate Analysis: Theory and Applications

Lauri Rapeli: The Conception of Citizen Knowledge in Democratic Theory

Michele Acuto and Simon Curtis: Reassembling International Theory: Assemblage Thinking and International Relations

Stephan Klingebiel: Development Cooperation: Challenges of the New Aid Architecture

DOI: 10.1057/9781137388575.0001

palgrave▸pivot

Contemporary Debates in Holocaust Education

Michael Gray

Researcher, Institute of Education, UK

DOI: 10.1057/9781137388575.0001

First published 2014 by
PALGRAVE MACMILLAN

Palgrave Macmillan in the UK is an imprint of Macmillan Publishers Limited, registered in England, company number 785998, of Houndmills, Basingstoke, Hampshire RG21 6XS.

Palgrave Macmillan in the US is a division of St Martin's Press LLC, 175 Fifth Avenue, New York, NY 10010.

Palgrave Macmillan is the global academic imprint of the above companies and has companies and representatives throughout the world.

Palgrave® and Macmillan® are registered trademarks in the United States, the United Kingdom, Europe and other countries.

ISBN: 978–1–137–38858–2 EPUB
ISBN: 978–1–137–38857–5 PDF
ISBN: 978–1–137–38856–8 Hardback

A catalogue record for this book is available from the British Library.

A catalog record for this book is available from the Library of Congress.

www.palgrave.com/pivot

DOI: 10.1057/9781137388575

Contents

Preface   vi

Acknowledgements   viii

List of Abbreviations   ix

1 Perceptions, Knowledge and Attitudes   1

2 Responses to Holocaust Education   21

3 The Quality of Research and Scholarship   42

4 Holocaust Universalisation   60

5 Teaching the Holocaust without Survivors   81

6 The Digital Era of Holocaust Education   99

Bibliography   115

Index   129

DOI: 10.1057/9781137388575.0001

Preface

In recent decades, Holocaust education has become an important part of the ever-expanding field of Holocaust studies. Across the globe, the systematic mass murder of the Jewish people is taught in schools, colleges, universities and beyond. Consequently, there has been a wealth of literature on what should be taught, how this should be done and what the aims and purposes of such an education ought to be. These debates have been continuing for a number of years and despite their important and valuable contribution, they seem to be reaching the point of scholarly exhaustion.

This publication aims to move forward the discussion by highlighting that debates within Holocaust education have gone beyond traditional and well-rehearsed arguments. Contemporary Holocaust pedagogy faces a number of practical challenges, such as student and teacher opposition, rising levels of anti-Semitism, the imminent passing of the survivor generation and the subject's increased trivialisation and universalisation. Yet in addition to the difficulties, various opportunities also exist as a consequence of developing technologies, social media and international collaboration. This book seeks to synthesise the most recent and innovative scholarship in these areas and to critically assess the arguments, research methods and conclusions which are drawn. It has been to the detriment of Holocaust education that such few attempts have been made to draw together the existing corpus of literature within the field and it is hoped that this effort to do so will somewhat contribute to this

DOI: 10.1057/9781137388575.0002

concerning omission. With one or two necessary exceptions, I have only drawn upon that which has been written in the English language. Despite both this and the ubiquity of Holocaust consciousness in North America, Western Europe and Israel, every effort has been made to adopt a truly global perspective.

DOI: 10.1057/9781137388575.0002

Acknowledgements

It is undoubtedly the case that this publication would not have been possible without the help and encouragement of various individuals and organisations along the way. Invaluable in my research has been a number of institutions including the Bodleian Library in Oxford, the Vaughan Library at Harrow School, the Wiener Library in London and the Newsam Library at the University of London's Institute of Education. The National Archives of the United Kingdom and the London Jewish Cultural Centre have also been kind enough to provide additional information, which has been of great help. Karen Van Coevorden at the Holocaust Educational Trust has graciously shared unpublished findings as has Jim Fanning, to whom I am extremely grateful. To my friends Ian Rowley and Chris Pollitt, for their help in translating text from French and German respectively, I am also most obliged.

I am especially grateful to Andrew James at Palgrave Macmillan for having faith in this project and for his vision in helping it become a reality. Professor Samuel Totten's constructive criticism was also invaluable in shaping the structure and content of this book.

Finally, I am indebted to my family, including my parents Peter and Wendy and my sister Rebecca. Most of all I owe my sincerest gratitude to my wife: Dr Angharad Gray, to whom this book is dedicated, for her wisdom, love and encouragement throughout the entire process. She has permitted me to discuss my ideas with her at length and been gracious and understanding in the countless hours which I have dedicated to the study of this macabre chapter of human history.

DOI: 10.1057/9781137388575.0003

List of Abbreviations

AFH	Anne Frank House
AJC	American Jewish Committee
CfHE	Centre for Holocaust Education (Formerly the Holocaust Education Development Programme)
FHAO	Facing History and Ourselves
HEDP	Holocaust Education Development Programme (Now the Centre for Holocaust Education)
HET	Holocaust Educational Trust
HMD	Holocaust Memorial Day
ICT	Information and Communications Technology
IHRA	International Holocaust Remembrance Alliance (formerly the International Task Force for International Cooperation on Holocaust Education, Remembrance and Research)
ITF	International Task Force for International Cooperation on Holocaust Education, Remembrance and Research (Now the International Holocaust Remembrance Alliance)
JESNA	Jewish Education Service of North America
NGO	Non-Governmental Organisation
ODIHR	Office for Democratic Institutions and Human Rights
PSHE	Personal Social Health Education
RS	Religious Studies
USC	University of Southern California
USHMM	United States Holocaust Memorial Museum

DOI: 10.1057/9781137388575.0004

palgrave▶**pivot**

www.palgrave.com/pivot

1
Perceptions, Knowledge and Attitudes

Abstract: *Research across the globe suggests that both students and teachers approach the subject of the Holocaust with ideological and historical preconceptions and that in some places knowledge of the topic is very limited indeed. Drawing on a number of studies from around the world, the relationship between ignorance and prejudice is explored as well as the way that attitudes and understandings can shape the nature of Holocaust education. Discussion is made concerning what ought to be considered as the expected standard of knowledge and whether existing scholarship has sometimes demanded too high a level of expertise from Holocaust educators.*

Keywords: anti-Semitism; attitudes; ignorance; knowledge; preconceptions; prejudice

Gray, Michael. *Contemporary Debates in Holocaust Education*. Basingstoke: Palgrave Macmillan, 2014. DOI: 10.1057/9781137388575.0005.

Connecting the two educational pillars of teaching and learning seems axiomatic. After all, how can effective teaching take place if there is no effective learning? Until recently, however, Holocaust education and certainly the scholarship within this particular field has typically focused on the teaching at the expense of the learning, or more precisely, the learner. Debates about the content of Holocaust curricula, the subject's uniqueness and the aims of teaching it have been important, and at times very productive, yet they have inadvertently marginalised the value of accounting for the learners; their preconceptions, attitudes, understandings and outlook.

Shemilt notes that 'programmes of history education should be informed by knowledge of how adolescents make sense of what is taught.'[1] This might be broadened even further and connected to notions of historical consciousness whereby 'those concerned with history education are looking beyond school for the ways in which the past figures in youngsters' views of the world',[2] both epistemologically and ontologically in a reciprocal, two-way relationship. In their valuable study for the National Research Council, Donovan and Bransford stated:

> Being learning-centred, then, involves paying attention to students' backgrounds and cultural values, as well as to their abilities. To build effectively on what learners bring to the classroom, teachers must pay close attention to individual students' starting points and to their progress on learning tasks.[3]

The relationship between what Rüsen calls *lebenspraxis* (practical life)[4] and more formalised education within the classroom is an important one. Relating this to Holocaust education involves understanding students' perceptions. What do they understand by terms such as 'concentration camp', 'Nazi' or 'Jew'? What attitudes and assumptions underpin these understandings? Moreover, what preconceptions about the Holocaust have students acquired before they formally study the subject in school? Of course, readjusting the focus to include the learner ought not to be at the expense of those teaching the learner. What are the perceptions, knowledge and attitudes of teachers? How much ought they to know about the Holocaust and how much do they know? To what extent do their prejudices and biases affect learners? These are some of the questions which studies are now beginning to address.

DOI: 10.1057/9781137388575.0005

Teachers' knowledge of the Holocaust

Many of the studies which have sought to measure or assess knowledge of the Holocaust have been carried out on random samples of the public. The American Jewish Committee (AJC), for example, surveyed about 1,000 people in each of Germany, Austria, France, Poland, Sweden, the United Kingdom and the United States of America. Despite some very poorly constructed questions in this study, it concluded that knowledge of the Holocaust is 'low and uneven in most countries'.[5] Jedwab's research on 1,500 Canadians concluded that 'just over 90% of Canadians surveyed are aware of the Holocaust'[6] while '65% of respondents agreed that they had good knowledge'.[7] Jedwab, however, did not test knowledge of the Holocaust but rather respondents' perceptions of their knowledge. This is somewhat problematic seeing that two individuals who have a different conception of what constitutes 'good knowledge' of the Holocaust may both consider that their knowledge is good when the levels of their knowledge may in fact be very different. Despite these concerns, Jedwab is right to bemoan the scarcity of studies which measure Holocaust knowledge and to call for a discussion about 'the minimal criteria to be considered adequately "informed" on the subject'.[8]

It would seem reasonable to argue that those teaching about the Holocaust ought to have greater knowledge than those who do not teach the subject. After all, as Lange states in his study of Swedish practitioners' perceptions and experiences of teaching the Holocaust:

> Teachers constitute an 'elite'. They are well-educated individuals who have been given – and have accepted – responsibility for a task that is of fundamental importance to society, namely that of conveying and facilitating the acquisition of basic knowledge and values among new generations of the members of society.[9]

Yet the existing evidence, limited though it is, certainly suggests that teachers' knowledge of the Holocaust is not satisfactory. Depending on how one interprets the data and the standard that is employed, there could even be a case to argue that the level of knowledge is woefully inadequate.

Out of the existing research, two major studies stand out as the most valuable and methodologically robust. The first of these was conducted by Lange on over 5,000 teachers in Sweden, the second by the Holocaust Education Development Programme (HEDP) on 2,108 teachers in

DOI: 10.1057/9781137388575.0005

England.[10] Although neither survey was principally exploring teachers' knowledge, both asked a series of relatively similar questions to respondents including what percentage of Germany's 1933 population consisted of Jews and questions that required knowledge of some of the specific camps which were used exclusively for the murdering of Jews. Lange had 11 questions in total which tested teachers' Holocaust knowledge, while the HEDP survey asked nine questions on the subject. The results appeared to demonstrate a distinct absence of knowledge. Lange wrote:

> Only 2 [of 508] teachers answered all of the questions correctly, and a further fourteen gave correct answers in relation to all but one of the questions. 7.8% answered all of the questions incorrectly, 27.8 answered all but one incorrectly, 26% gave two correct answers and 16.6% gave three correct answers. Thus 70.4% of the respondents gave incorrect answers to at least eight of the eleven questions.[11]

Foster, the Director of the HEDP, found similar results.

> Only 48 of the 1,816 (2.6%) teachers who responded to the online questionnaire answered all the questions correctly where 687 teachers (37.8%) either provided one or no correct answer to any of the questions.[12]

Lange acknowledges that 'testing teachers' knowledge – irrespective of the type of knowledge in question – is a problematic venture',[13] while Foster too states that 'mapping knowledge in any subject is an inherently complex undertaking' and thus 'it would be imprudent to make sweeping generalisations about teachers' subject knowledge'.[14] It is difficult to know whether Lange and the HEDP, in their respective studies, would expect the majority of their respondents to provide the correct answer to the majority of the questions posed. If so, then this is very intellectually demanding and while it is useful to begin to establish an agreed benchmark for what is 'adequate knowledge' for a teacher to hold, this particular model perhaps seems too challenging. It must be taken into account that teachers are not expected to be Holocaust specialists and that this is just one part of what is often a very large curriculum. With that in mind, asking them the specific name attributed to the Nazi genocide of the Roma[15] and whether or not Roosevelt was the only leader to publicly condemn the events of *Kristallnacht* seems to be a very high standard.[16] Moreover, many of the respondents were not history teachers. Jedwab perceptively notes:

> Of the empirical studies conducted to date, observers have been surprised by just how many people report limited or no awareness of the Holocaust.

DOI: 10.1057/9781137388575.0005

Perhaps this is because leaders in the field of Holocaust education set the bar too high when it comes to the desired level of knowledge.[17]

The results of the Holocaust knowledge questions within these two major studies do, however, demonstrate some very interesting findings. For example, in the HEDP research, those with greater knowledge of the Holocaust were more likely to emphasise the specificity of the targeting of the Jews while those with the least knowledge were most likely to understand the Holocaust as a phenomenon involving a wide range of victims.[18] Lange's findings concluded that Holocaust knowledge was highest among 55–60-year-old teachers. He also found that 56.7 per cent of teachers felt that their knowledge of the Holocaust could be 'somewhat or much better'[19] while in the HEDP survey, most teachers in all subjects felt confident in their knowledge.[20]

Moving beyond Sweden and England, many researchers have noted the lack of Holocaust knowledge which is demonstrated by teachers. While most of their comments are drawn from anecdotal evidence rather than empirical surveys, they do provide something of an insight into what remains an under-researched field. Nates, for example, in her work with South African teachers wrote that 'educators have little or no knowledge of the Holocaust.'[21] She went onto state that 'there are hundreds of thousands of educators and learners who have very little knowledge of the complex history of the Holocaust.'[22] These summations were based on experiences at teacher training workshops where South African educators were given mind-maps to find out how much they knew about the Holocaust. Moreover, Nates comments, 'when asked to identify different countries on a European map, almost all educators without exception, cannot find Germany, Poland or the Netherlands.'[23]

Morocco, like South Africa, is a country where the Holocaust has not been a part of national consciousness. Polak notes that 'until now there has been little, if any, public knowledge of this history, and perhaps a certain amount of resistance to such teaching.'[24] Yet the Moroccan government's Ministry of Education, in contrast to many of its North African neighbours, is actively pursuing programmes and initiatives which will help to educate their teachers on Holocaust and human rights education.

In contrast, the major report, *Education on the Holocaust and on Anti-Semitism*, conducted by the Office for Democratic Institutions and Human Rights (ODIHR), noted that one of the most common obstacles for teaching the Holocaust within Europe was the 'lack of adequate

DOI: 10.1057/9781137388575.0005

teacher preparation' and 'the lack of adequate funding... for teacher training'.[25] In the 2006 report by the Jewish Education Service of North America (JESNA), 22 leading professionals in American Holocaust education were interviewed. They commonly agreed that within the US, 'teachers are not trained well enough in the history itself and its complexity' and that 'teachers lack knowledge of the methodologies and pedagogic strategies to deliver that history'.[26] This suggests that teachers' levels of knowledge may sometimes be a limitation on the quality of the Holocaust education that is being delivered.

Gross's work in Poland would support this idea. Her study of 60 teachers who participated in a Holocaust teacher programme found that practitioners' knowledge of the subject was often a significant problem. One of the respondents in the research believed that 'the biggest barrier to Holocaust education is the lack of professional and material support for teachers, and that teachers suffered from a lack of knowledge about the Holocaust and Jewish culture in Poland'.[27]

Misco's work in Latvia also highlighted a deficiency in the aptitude and understanding of the Holocaust among its educators. In his study of 50 teachers, one of the six reasons he elicited as to why the Holocaust is marginalised and often ignored within Latvian schools was 'lack of knowledge'.[28] Misco writes:

> Additional issues that serve to minimize teaching, learning and talking about the Holocaust are lack of knowledge and apathy. Although apathy can certainly be tied to Latvian victimization, whereby concern for those other than Latvians is diminished, it also stems from ignorance on the topic. Lack of knowledge about the Holocaust, which was promulgated during the Soviet era and still influences generations of Latvians, has only diminished partially.[29]

To a limited extent the situation above is also true of Romania where 'a prominent legacy of the communist-era is the general lack of knowledge about the Holocaust'.[30] Yet seemingly in contrast to Latvia:

> For the past few years, Romanian educators have refined their knowledge and understanding of Holocaust education, including a substantial number of domestic and international teacher in-services and a proliferation of books and materials on the subject.[31]

The potential inadequacy of teacher knowledge on the Holocaust and the deficiency of training opportunities do not appear to be the case in Israel. Cohen's major study of Holocaust education in Israel conducted

DOI: 10.1057/9781137388575.0005

on 2,540 students, 519 teachers and 307 principals allows for a clearer picture of the state of Holocaust education here than in perhaps any other country. He noted that 'the people teaching the Shoah in Israeli schools are highly educated and experienced. Virtually all the teachers hold at least a bachelor's degree and almost half earned a master's degree ... most have received at least some specialized training in teaching the Shoah.'[32] Cohen goes onto say that 'the wide availability of enrichment courses specifically geared towards teaching the Shoah is another distinguishing feature of the Israeli educational landscape',[33] with courses being offered by Yad Vashem, the Ministry of Education, as well as various other museums and institutions.

Overall, it must be acknowledged that on the basis of such minimal research around the world, it is impossible to adequately summarise teachers' knowledge of the Holocaust without resorting to gross generalisations. Undoubtedly there are significant differences between countries, regions and even institutions. Nevertheless, one may tentatively suggest from the existing corpus of scholarship, that in some countries in particular, there is a need to raise the levels of existing knowledge. It seems highly unlikely that there will be an agreed body of knowledge for teachers any time soon. Nevertheless, greater consensus on what teachers ought to be expected to know is needed; at present it seems that practitioners and academics are divergent on what ought to be expected from educators. Moreover, it seems apparent that further research needs to be conducted in this particular field of Holocaust education if teacher training is to target the precise areas where knowledge needs to improve.

Students' knowledge of the Holocaust

Many of the same problems and challenges which exist in assessing the levels of teachers' knowledge are also applicable when exploring students' knowledge of the Holocaust. What exactly should adolescents know and what constitutes 'adequate' or even 'commendable' levels of knowledge? While both scholars[34] and many of the major Holocaust organisations such as the United States Holocaust Memorial Museum (USHMM), amongst others, have suggested what ought to be included in a Holocaust curriculum, there remains a lack of consensus. Moreover, to what depth ought these topics to be taught and how is understanding, as well as knowledge, most appropriately measured?

DOI: 10.1057/9781137388575.0005

Examining students' knowledge of the Holocaust after they have been taught the subject is to some extent at least measuring the effectiveness of the teacher in delivering the course and the ability of the student to recall information. It is thus more insightful to explore what adolescents know and understand about the Holocaust *before* they have studied it formally in school. This involves discovering their preconceptions; what ideas they have acquired about the subject from films, books, the internet, friends or school. Schweber anecdotally comments:

> I suspect that most kids in the United States first learn about the Holocaust, slavery, and other atrocities in history accidentally, randomly, because they happened to be standing by the monkey bars in the school playground on a Thursday morning.[35]

How pupils typically first hear about the Holocaust is difficult to gauge, but what is increasingly apparent is that many pupils are acquiring conceptions and knowledge of the subject from an early age.[36] In a study directed by Cohen in 2009 on students in American Junior High and High schools, 99 per cent of them had heard of the Holocaust before they learnt about it in the curriculum.[37] Consequently, it is imperative that teachers explore pupils' prior thinking so that they can challenge misconceptions, build on existing ideas and adjust their curriculum to tackle specific areas of ignorance. Totten writes:

> Experience has taught me that a study of the Holocaust which begins with an examination of what students know, don't know, and want to know ultimately contributes to a more potent and meaningful understanding of this tragic event.[38]

Yet despite this, the numbers of studies which have specifically explored pupils' intellectual preconceptions have been few, with far more research choosing to focus on attitudes and feelings than on knowledge and understanding. To some extent one ought not to draw too much of a distinction, for knowledge and attitudes are certainly connected and studies which have sought to explore pupils' understandings have often commented on attitudes in order to contextualise and make sense of their data.

In Ivanova's important research conducted on 15–17-year-olds in Ukraine, she studied both pupils' knowledge and attitudes. One hundred and seven adolescents were each given a sheet of paper with the statement, 'Please write about the Holocaust (the mass extermination of the Jews during the Second World War).' This open-ended activity did not place limitations on what pupils knew by asking precisely selected, closed-ended questions. It also provided respondents with the opportunity to express those elements of the Holocaust which they felt were particularly important or pertinent. Although all of the pupils had previously studied the Second World War, Ivanova observed that textbooks offered very limited information on the Holocaust. The findings suggested a significant deficiency in knowledge and understanding of the subject.

> Many had not really heard about the Holocaust and, according to several students at one of the schools, it had not even been mentioned in their history lessons. It was obvious how difficult it was for the youngsters to write anything on the subject.[39]

Ivanova also noted that 'fewer than 10 per cent of the students were able to articulate significant historical knowledge',[40] with the majority of those individuals coming from a Jewish school. Yet connected to this ignorance was the attitude of some of the respondents, with 11 per cent of those from the non-Jewish school expressing an openly anti-Semitic discourse.[41]

The relationship between a lack of knowledge and anti-Semitism is also demonstrated in Gross's work conducted on 60 teachers in Poland. She noted that 'fifty-eight per cent of the teachers stated that students came to school with a general lack of knowledge about Jews' and that 'sixty per cent stated that their students arrived with stereotypes or negative attitudes about the Jews'.[42] Unsurprisingly therefore, when constructing a list of the obstacles to teaching about the Holocaust in Poland, teachers placed stereotypes and negatives attitudes of the Jews as the primary limitation and students' lack of knowledge as the second largest obstacle.[43]

The seeming ignorance of adolescents in Ukraine and Poland is also mirrored in other parts of Europe. Misco records the comments of an experienced Latvian teacher, for example, who noted, 'I saw it clearly that children don't have any idea.'[44] Elsewhere, Misco writes that 'Romanian students' knowledge about the Holocaust is sometimes incomplete, biased, or cursory.'[45] If such are Romanian students' preconceptions, it does not bode well when Misco also records that 'when asked what students would actually learn about the Holocaust in the normal curriculum, one prominent history inspector suggested "almost nothing".'[46]

In Slovakia, Michaels acknowledges the different discourses which underpin and influence the direction of Holocaust education and consequently the knowledge acquired by students. In her valuable analysis of Slovakia's prescriptive textbooks she observes that although 'textbooks and curricular documents should not be simplistically equated with teacher practice or student beliefs ... Students who wish to successfully advance through the academic system must possess knowledge of this material, even if they do not believe its content or ideological message.'[47] This highlights the importance of recognising that the nature of adolescents' Holocaust knowledge is just as important as the quantity. Moreover, students may possess ideas and information about the subject in preparation for an exam without necessarily believing it. In addition, they may have neither the time nor the inclination to challenge the prevailing orthodoxy of mainstream national discourses. Conversely, Frankl's assessment of Holocaust education in the neighbouring Czech Republic found that in the post-Soviet years there had been considerable advances and that many of the contemporary teaching resources focused on detailed historical knowledge, perhaps at the expense of helping practitioners how to teach the subject.[48] This suggests that factual and accurate information on the Holocaust is readily available for both teachers and students. Nevertheless, if teachers are not sufficiently equipped to make the subject interesting or relevant, then many adolescents may not wish to acquire the knowledge that is available.

Santerini argues that in Italy, like in so many other countries, Holocaust education is 'indissolubly connected' to the country's historical memory.[49] Yet unless cultural memory prevails over political memory, 'Holocaust education runs the risk of being seen as irrelevant.'[50] The logical outcome of this would not only be a decrease in students' prior knowledge of the subject but a reduction in their motivation and desire to know and understand.

As discussed in Chapter 2, Holocaust education cannot be detached from national consciousness and memory. It therefore seems apparent that students' awareness and understanding of the Holocaust is reduced in countries where the subject is not a significant part of its national memory and identity or where that national memory is selective in its use of the Holocaust. Similarly, in places where the Holocaust, and all aspects of it, is an important tenet of a country's identity and history, either directly or indirectly, one might expect knowledge of the subject to be higher. This appears to be the case. In Germany, for example, Welzer argues that young people learn about Nazi Germany and the Holocaust, not simply through formal education but, perhaps more importantly,

DOI: 10.1057/9781137388575.0005

through 'the emotional wallop of images from the past offered by most other sources'.[51] He also states that in Germany 'survey data show that young Germans are generally quite well informed about the historical events and can associate correctly with keywords such as "Auschwitz" and "SS".'[52]

It seems that the Holocaust plays no more of an important role in national consciousness than in Israel. Cohen discovered that 'three quarters of the students and virtually all of the teachers (96%) said that the Shoah influences their world view'.[53] Yet the same might also be said of Jews within the Diaspora. In a study conducted in 2008 of over a thousand French Jewish youth, 92 per cent stated that their worldview was affected by the Holocaust, which was in fact higher than Jewish youth in Israel.[54]

Despite the fact that according to Auron, 'the Holocaust is studied more in Israel – apparently very much more – than any other subject in the field of modern Jewish history',[55] Cohen found that 83 per cent of students wanted to learn more about it. He also presented compelling evidence to support the idea that Israeli students' knowledge of the Holocaust is vast and almost universal. Amongst 12th grade students, 98 per cent of them had familiarity and recognition of the term 'ghetto', 97 per cent with both Kristallnacht and Janusz Korczak, 93 per cent with Judenräte, 90 per cent with the Wannsee Conference and 88 per cent with the Molotov-Ribbentrop pact.[56]

Studies on adolescents' preconceptions in England have also highlighted that many of them have considerable knowledge of the Holocaust before they formally learn about it at school. According to the HEDP report on Holocaust education in England, the subject is most commonly taught when pupils are aged 13 and 14. In a sample of 26 boys, Edwards and O'Dowd found a wide range of preconceptions, some idiosyncratic in nature, but with most pupils demonstrating some meaningful historical knowledge and understanding. They concluded that the 'class's prior knowledge of events varied in levels of complexity' but that 'in a few cases understandings were detailed and in most cases they showed a familiarity with some of the main events'.[57] While the lack of data makes international comparison impossible, a more detailed look at the results of Edwards and O'Dowd's study suggest that in this small sample there was significant and meaningful knowledge with over half the class recognising the Star of David and many students stating that extermination had been preceded by persecution.

DOI: 10.1057/9781137388575.0005

With a sample of 298 13-year-olds from four different English schools, Gray also explored students' knowledge and understanding of the Holocaust before they had formally studied the subject in their History curriculum.[58] He specifically noted the influence of certain books and films on adolescents' thinking, notably *Anne Frank: The Diary of a Young Girl* and especially *The Boy in the Striped Pyjamas*. Gray also found that many respondents provided Hitler-centric explanations of the Holocaust and erroneously perceived that the Nazis defined Jews in religious rather than racial terms. Although there were common misconceptions regarding the geography and scale of the Holocaust, almost all students had detailed knowledge about various elements of the camps and the nature of living conditions within them. Virtually every student lacked knowledge of the ghettos and the role of the *Einsatzgruppen*, seeming to believe that all Jews who perished at the hands of the Nazis experienced a near identical experience, in that they were taken from their homes to concentration camps where they were either gassed or shot. Yet a workable understanding, based on reasonable knowledge, was possessed by the vast majority of students, that being *before* they had studied the subject in school.

Instead of focusing on historical knowledge of the Holocaust, a qualitative study conducted by Short analysed students' knowledge and understanding of the *moral lessons* of the Holocaust, stating that 'knowledge of how the Holocaust is relevant to contemporary life (both locally and globally) has to be seen as a necessary condition of successful Holocaust education.'[59] Short interviewed 31 pupils from London schools who came from a wide range of backgrounds, but had all participated in a specific Holocaust Memorial Day (HMD) event. He noted that for the majority of those who participated in the experience, they had perceived the only benefits to be an increase in their historical knowledge of the subject and that 'overall, the students failed to learn a number of important lessons from the Holocaust and the events that led to it'.[60] Short therefore concluded that most students were not able to draw out lessons from the Holocaust by themselves and that the respondents' teachers may also have failed to do so. Though Short's beliefs about what constitutes successful Holocaust education are not shared by all teachers – many of whom actively resist the notion of acquiring moral lessons from the past – it does offer a different dimension to the sort of knowledge which ought to be measured and analysed. Yet it is important to note that historical knowledge and 'moral knowledge' are connected. While

DOI: 10.1057/9781137388575.0005

the former can exist independently of the latter, it seems unlikely that meaningful lessons can be drawn if there is no historical basis. After all, without grounding any 'moral knowledge' in its historical context almost any lesson whatsoever can be drawn.

Attitudes towards the Holocaust among teachers and students

In addition to exploring the nature and extent of both teachers' and students' knowledge, empirical studies (either intentionally or not) have also shed light on some of the attitudes that exist within Holocaust education. It is unsurprising that the subject can generate a wide array of attitudes, ranging from enthusiasm and fascination to opposition and detachment. Responses to Holocaust education are discussed in Chapter 2 and thus the briefer discussion here is principally confined to the relationship between attitudes and knowledge.

The principal relationship is that attitudes towards the Holocaust are connected to the depth of historical knowledge and understanding which is held by the learner. Those with particularly negative attitudes towards the subject are often those with the least awareness of the details of the Holocaust as a historical phenomenon. In Ivanova's study of Ukrainian students where ignorance appeared endemic, she also observed virulent and aggressive anti-Semitism. One respondent wrote of the Jews, 'They all need to be rooted out...I think you can't ignore this plague, which is swarming worldwide – they have to be exterminated!', while another stated, 'Hitler killed many Jews. Way to go!'.[61]

In a study by Maitles and Cowan in Scotland, knowledge of the Holocaust was cross-referenced with children's attitudes towards Jews.[62] They found that racist attitudes were more likely to emerge from those without knowledge of the Holocaust. Although these findings would support other studies, the validity of the link is somewhat suspect. Maitles and Cowan considered the sample section as having 'knowledge' simply if they perceived that they knew what the Holocaust was. Moreover, there were only four pupils out of 133 who agreed that it was acceptable to make racist statements about the Jews.[63]

More valuable is Kelso's large-scale study of over 600 teachers in Romania between 2005 and 2010, which also supports the idea that there are important links between knowledge and attitudes. Yet unlike

DOI: 10.1057/9781137388575.0005

in the studies by Gross, Ivanova, and Maitles and Cowan, the ignorance was held by teachers and not students. Furthermore, the target of the prejudice and intolerance was not Jews but Roma. Irrespective of these differences, the correlation between a lack of knowledge and a lack of acceptance continues to be evident. In evaluating Holocaust education in Romania, Kelso makes the connection by stating that 'ignorance about the Holocaust and prejudice about the minorities affected are at the root of non-compliance in teaching.'[64] Although 'the majority of teachers in this study demonstrated a lack of historical and cultural knowledge about the Roma',[65] Kelso highlights their willingness to make generalised comments about them such as 'Roma do not want to integrate into society', 'Roma steal things and are violent' and 'Roma do not want to be educated'.[66]

It is perhaps especially worrying when the traits of ignorance and prejudice are found in teachers. In many countries it is individual practitioners who determine whether Holocaust education is going to be a superficial exercise or a meaningful study. Moreover, it seems very difficult for teachers to educate their students when they are deficient of the requisite knowledge. What seems more likely is that their prejudices will be transmitted instead of the historical understanding which it was their duty to provide.

Tackling the ignorance and prejudice which are characterised in the findings of the likes of Ivanova, Gross and Kelso represent a major challenge. This is principally because the two concepts support each other. The prejudice that individuals hold make them reluctant to learn more about the subject and in some cases reject new information which challenge their misconceptions. Kelso for example observed how many Romanian teachers were unwilling to integrate new research on the Roma into their existing frameworks of thinking or even include the Roma in their teaching of the Holocaust.

> I found that teachers' resistance to incorporating Roma into Holocaust education results from ignorance (wilful or otherwise) of the events surrounding the Holocaust in Romania and deep-seated (historical and contemporary) prejudice against the Romani minority in Romania.[67]

Yet in addition to the prejudice supporting ignorance, so the latter buttresses the former, for prejudicial ideas can be self-justified when supported by one's internal logic. Ignorance prevents this quasi-logic from being dismantled. Kelso also noted that 'teachers could not detach contemporary prejudices of Roma with their understandings of the past.'[68]

DOI: 10.1057/9781137388575.0005

Ignorance and prejudice seems to be apparent, often to a limited extent in much of the research conducted on teachers and students. Gray's study of 147 pupils in England, for example, concluded that 'for all the endeavours and education that teachers give and pupils receive, there is still the persistence of myths, prejudices and important historical inaccuracies.'[69] Schweber noted in her qualitative study *Simulating Survival,* 'two of the four students I interviewed... had held negative associations with the word "Jew" at the beginning of the semester.'[70] In a study of over 200 pupils' values and attitudes in Scotland, Maitles and Cowan found that over 10 per cent of the sample believed that there were too many Jews in Scotland and approximately 2 per cent thought it was 'ok for adults to make racist comments about Jewish people.'[71] Despite this, Maitles and Cowan also noted the enthusiasm for learning about the Holocaust with fewer than 15 per cent disagreeing with the statements that they should learn more about the subject and would like to find out more.[72]

Yet attitudes towards Jews, as well as teaching and learning about the Holocaust, are by no means all negative; in many cases they are quite the contrary. Gray reported examples of pupils in England sometimes demonstrating philosemitism.[73] In interviews conducted by Short with various 14 to 16-year-olds in England, one student stated:

> What I thought before and what I think now has definitely changed. Before [HMD] Jewish people to me were just seen as normal people, but after HMD I think these people have been persecuted so much. They went through the Holocaust with so much pride, I think there's a lot to learn from Jewish people these days.[74]

Moreover, in his study on Swedish teachers Lange reported that 44 per cent believed that the Holocaust was more interesting to study than other topics.[75] Likewise, 'an overwhelming majority of the teachers – 93.8 percent – reported that the students are quite interested (51.7 percent) or very interested (42 percent) in the subject.'[76] A study of teachers in Ontario, Canada also found that there was enthusiasm for the significance of the subject.[77] The overwhelming popularity and impact of Holocaust literature throughout the world in many different languages is also testament to the interest of young people in the subject. This includes *The Boy in the Striped Pyjamas*[78] as well as *Anne Frank: The Diary of a Young Girl* which was recently translated into Arabic.[79]

Within the United States of America, there have been a number of studies which have analysed the effectiveness of the commonly used curriculum 'Facing History and Ourselves' (FHAO) in challenging

DOI: 10.1057/9781137388575.0005

stereotypes and tackling prejudices. Morse, in a study of 92 students in three American schools found that completing the FHAO course did not have a significant quantifiable effect.[80] Bardige too, using the journals of students taking the FHAO course, found that the 'moral development revealed by these journals could not be characterized as either movement to or towards a new "stage," or within-stage increases in empathy and social responsibility'.[81] Riley, Washington and Humphries, in their thoughtful and critical overview of FHAO, note that Lowenstein,[82] in the most recent thesis exploring the impact of 'Facing History and Ourselves', concluded that the programme 'made only a limited impact in most cases' on teachers' beliefs about citizenship and civics education.[83] Yet a study conducted by Schultz, Barr and Selman on FHAO, for example, did conclude that students who participated in a ten-week FHAO curriculum demonstrated increases in relationship maturity and decreases in racist attitudes. Nevertheless, the moral reasoning and civic attitudes of the 212 adolescents who took part in the FHAO course was not significantly greater than the 134 comparison students.[84]

In a different political context, using a different curriculum, Ene's study of secondary school students in Northern Greece found that by adopting an interdisciplinary approach, which made use of art, drama, personal testimonies and visits to sites and museums, 'there was a significant progress not only in the knowledge acquired by the students on the Holocaust but also an evident change in their opinions on issues concerning racial superiority, social discrimination, tolerance and acceptance of the other'.[85] In assessing various curricula, including FHAO, carefully constructed studies which measure the long-term implications over several years are needed rather than an over-reliance on simple pre- and post-curriculum surveys.

Discovering attitudes, knowledge and perceptions is always a difficult task, perhaps made even more challenging in the field of Holocaust education due to the inherent complexity of the subject matter. Nevertheless, the existing scholarship indicates that while in some parts of the world enthusiasm for studying the Holocaust remains high, in other places there appears significant prejudice and anti-Semitism. Successfully tackling ignorance and prejudice, as well as the relationship between the two, remains one of the biggest challenges for contemporary Holocaust education.

DOI: 10.1057/9781137388575.0005

Notes

1   Shemilt, D. (2006) 'The Future of the Past: How Adolescents make Sense of Past, Present and Future'. Paper presented the International Invitation Conference: *National History Standards: The Problem of the Canon and the Future of History Teaching*, University of Utrecht, October 2006, p. 2.

2   Lee, P. (2004) ' "Walking Backwards into Tomorrow": Historical Consciousness and Understanding History', *International Journal of Historical Learning, Teaching and Research*, 4: 1, 1–46, p. 2.

3   Donovan, M. S. and Bransford, J. D. (2005) 'Introduction', in M. S. Donovan and J. D. Bransford (Ed.) *How Students Learn. History in the Classroom*, (Washington DC: National Academies Press), p. 14.

4   Rüsen, J. (1990) *Zeit und Sinn: Strategien historischen Denkens*, (Frankfurt: Am Main).

5   Harris, D. (2005) 'Foreword', in Smith, T (Ed.) *The Holocaust and its Implications: A Seven-Nation Comparative Study*, (New York: American Jewish Committee), p. 6.

6   Jedwab, J. (2010) 'Measuring Holocaust Knowledge and its Impact: A Canadian Case Study', *Prospects*, 40: 2, 273–287, p. 286.

7   Jedwab, 'Measuring Holocaust Knowledge', p. 278.

8   Jedwab, 'Measuring Holocaust Knowledge', p. 286.

9   Lange, A. (2008) *A Survey of Teachers' Experiences and Perceptions in Relation to Teaching about the Holocaust*, (Stockholm: Living History Forum), p. 67.

10   Pettigrew, A., Foster, S., Howson, J., Salmons, P., Lenga, R- A. and Andrews, K. (2009) *Teaching about the Holocaust in English Secondary Schools: An Empirical Study of National Trends, Perspectives and Practice*, (Holocaust Education Development Programme, Institute of Education, University of London).

11   Lange, *A Survey of Teachers' Experiences*, p. 73.

12   Foster, S. (2013) 'Teaching about the Holocaust in English Schools: Challenges and Possibilities', *Intercultural Education*, 24: 1–2, pp. 133–148, p. 139.

13   Lange, *A Survey of Teachers' Experiences*, p. 67.

14   Foster, 'Teaching about the Holocaust', p. 139.

15   Question V108 in Lange, *A Survey of Teachers' Experiences*, p. 101.

16   Question 28 in HEDP, 'Teaching about the Holocaust', p. 112.

17   Jedwab, 'Measuring Holocaust Knowledge', p. 274.

18   Pettigrew et al., *Teaching about the Holocaust*, p. 68.

19   Lange, *A Survey of Teachers' Experiences*, p. 60.

20   Pettigrew et al., *Teaching about the Holocaust*, p. 47.

21   Nates, T. (2010) ' "But, Apartheid was also Genocide ... What about our Suffering?" Teaching the Holocaust in South Africa – Opportunities and Challenges', *Intercultural Education*, 21: S1, S17–S26, p. S22.

DOI: 10.1057/9781137388575.0005

22 Nates, 'But Apartheid was also Genocide', p. S24.

23 Nates, 'But Apartheid was also Genocide', p. S22.

24 Polak, K. (2010) 'Tolerance Education in Morocco. "Anne Frank: A History for Today": Learning about our Past – Contributing to our Future', *Intercultural Education*, 21: S1, S51–S59, p. S51.

25 Office for Democratic Institutions and Human Rights. (2005) *Education on the Holocaust and on Anti-Semitism*, p. 36.

26 Isaacs, L., Rosov, W., Raff, L., Rosenblatt, S., Hecht, S., Rozenek, M. and Rotem, Z. (2006) 'Best Practices in Holocaust Education': Report to the San Francisco Jewish Community Endowment Fund, Jewish Education Service of North America, p. 16.

27 Gross, Z. and Stevick E. D. (2010) 'Holocaust Education – International Perspectives: Challenges, Opportunities and Research', *Prospects*, 40: 1, 17–33, p. 109.

28 Misco, T. (2011) ' "Most Learn almost Nothing": Building Democratic Citizenship by Engaging Controversial History through Inquiry in Post-Communist Europe', *Education, Citizenship, and Social Justice*, 6: 1, 87–104, p. 91.

29 Misco, 'Most Learn Almost Nothing', p. 93.

30 Misco, 'Most Learn Almost Nothing', p. 96.

31 Misco, 'Most Learn Almost Nothing', p. 95.

32 Cohen, E. (2013) *Identity and Pedagogy: Shoah Education in Israeli State Schools*, (Brighton, MA: Academic Studies Press), p. 97.

33 Cohen, *Identity and Pedagogy*, p. 98.

34 Glanz, J. (1999) 'Ten Suggestions for Teaching the Holocaust', *The History Teacher*, 32: 4, 547–565; Friedländer, H. (1980) 'Towards a Methodology of Teaching about the Holocaust', in Friedlander, H. and Milton, S. (Eds) *The Holocaust: Ideology, Bureaucracy and Genocide*, The San Jose Papers, The National Conference of Christians and Jews, 1980.

35 Schweber, S. (2008) ' "What Happened to their Pets?": Third Graders Encounter the Holocaust', *Teachers College Record*, 110: 10, p. 2074.

36 See Schweber, 'What Happened to their Pets?'.

37 Cohen, E. (2009) *Echoes and Reflections 2008-2009*. Yad Vashem and ADL. Unpublished Report.

38 Totten, S. (1998) 'The Start is as Important as the Finish', *Social Education*, 62: 2, 70–76, p. 76.

39 Ivanova, E. (2004) 'Ukrainian High School Students' Understanding of the Holocaust', *Holocaust and Genocide Studies*, 18: 3, 402–420, p. 407.

40 Ivanova, 'Ukrainian High School', p. 407.

41 Ivanova, 'Ukrainian High School', p. 408.

42 Gross, M. (2013) 'To Teach the Holocaust in Poland: Understanding Teachers' Motivations to Engage the Painful Past', *Intercultural Education*, 24: 1–2, 103–120, p. 112.

DOI: 10.1057/9781137388575.0005

43   Gross, 'To Teach the Holocaust', p. 112.

44   Misco, 'Most Learn Almost Nothing', p. 93.

45   Misco, T. (2008) ' "We did also save People": A Study of Holocaust Education in Romania after Decades of Historical Silence', *Theory and Research in Social Education*, 36: 2, 61–94, p. 62.

46   Misco, 'Most Learn Almost Nothing', p. 96.

47   Michaels, D. (2013) 'Holocaust Education in the "Black Hole of Europe": Slovakia's Identity Politics and History Textbooks Pre- and Post- 1989', *Intercultural Education*, 24: 1–2, 19–40, p. 23.

48   Frankl, M. (2003) 'Holocaust Education in the Czech Republic, 1989–2002', *Intercultural Education*, 14: 2, 177–189, p. 187.

49   Santerini, M. (2003) 'Holocaust Education in Italy', *Intercultural Education*, 14: 2, 225–232, p. 225.

50   Santerini, 'Holocaust Education in Italy', p. 229.

51   Welzer, H. (2008) 'Collateral Damage of History Education: National Socialism and the Holocaust in German Family Memory', *Social Research*, 75: 1, 287–314, p. 288–289.

52   Welzer, 'Collateral Damage of History Education', p. 288.

53   Cohen, *Identity and Pedagogy*, p. 153.

54   Cohen, E. (2008) *Youth Tourism to Israel: Educational Experiences of the Diaspora*, (Clevedon UK: Channel View Publications).

55   Auron, Y. (2003) *The Pain of Knowledge: Holocaust and Genocide Issues in Education*, (London: Transaction Publishers), p. 74.

56   Cohen, *Identity and Pedagogy*, pp. 182–183.

57   Edwards, C. and O'Dowd, S. (2010) 'The Edge of Knowing: Investigating Students' Prior Understandings of the Holocaust', *Teaching History*, 141, 20–26, p. 22.

58   Gray, M. (2014) *Preconceptions of the Holocaust among Thirteen and Fourteen year olds in English Schools*. Unpublished PhD Thesis, Centre for Holocaust Education, Institute of Education, University of London (Forthcoming).

59   Short, G. (2005) 'Learning from Genocide? A Study in the Failure of Holocaust Education', *Intercultural Education*, 16: 4, 367–380, p. 378.

60   Short, 'Learning from Genocide?', p. 377.

61   Ivanova, 'Ukrainian High School', pp. 408–409.

62   Maitles, H., Cowan, P. and Butler, E. (2006) 'Never Again!: Does Holocaust Education have an Effect on Pupils' Citizenship Values and Attitudes?', Scottish Executive Social Research.

63   Maitles, Cowan and Butler, 'Never Again', p. 29.

64   Kelso, M. (2013) ' "And Roma were Victims too." ' The Romani Genocide and Holocaust Education in Romania', *Intercultural Education*, 24, 1–2, 61–78, p. 61.

65   Kelso, 'And Roma were Victims too', p.70.

DOI: 10.1057/9781137388575.0005

66   Kelso, 'And Roma were Victims too', p. 67.

67   Kelso, 'And Roma were Victims too', p. 70.

68   Kelso, 'And Roma were Victims too', p. 67.

69   Gray, M. (2013) 'Exploring Pupil Perceptions of Jews, Jewish Identity and the Holocaust', *Journal of Modern Jewish Studies* 12: 3, p. 11.

70   Schweber, S. (2003) 'Simulating Survival', *Curriculum Inquiry*, 33: 2, 139–188, p. 179.

71   Maitles, Cowan and Butler, 'Never Again!', p. 28.

72   Maitles, Cowan and Butler, 'Never Again!', p. 35.

73   Gray, 'Exploring Pupil Perceptions'.

74   Short, 'Learning from Genocide?', p. 376.

75   Lange, *A Survey of Teachers' Experiences*, p. 61.

76   Lange, *A Survey of Teachers' Experiences*, p. 61.

77   Cohen-Almagor, R. (2008) 'Hate in the Classroom: Free Expression, Holocaust Denial, and Liberal Education'. *American Journal of Education*, 114, 215–241.

78   Gray, 'Understanding Pupil Preconceptions', p. 16.

79   Davis, B. and Rubinstein-Avila, E. (2013) 'Holocaust Education: Global Forces Shaping Curricula Integration and Implementation', *Intercultural Education*, 24: 1–2, 149–166, p. 158.

80   Morse, D. (1981) *Studying the Holocaust and Human Behaviour: Effects on Early Adolescent Self-Esteem, Locus of Control, Acceptance of Self and Others, and Philosophy of Human Nature*, Unpublished Dissertation, Boston College.

81   Bardige, B. (1983) *Reflective Thinking and Prosocial Awareness: Adolescents Face the Holocaust and Themselves.* Unpublished Dissertation. Harvard University, p. 195.

82   Lowenstein, E. (2003) *Teachers Transformed? Exploring the Influence of Facing History and Ourselves on Teachers' Beliefs about Citizenship and Civics Education.* Unpublished Dissertation. New York University.

83   Riley, K., Washington, E. and Humphries, E. (2011) 'Facing History and Ourselves: Noble Purpose, Unending Controversy', in Totten, S. and Pedersen, J. (Eds) *Teaching and Studying Social Issues: Major Programs and Approaches*, (Charlotte, North Carolina: Information Age Publishing), pp. 119–139, p. 127.

84   Schultz, L., Barr, D. and Selman, R. (2001) 'The Value of a Developmental Approach to Evaluating Character Development Programmes: An Outcome Study of Facing History and Ourselves', *Journal of Moral Education*, 30: 1, 3–27.

85   Ene, C. (2013) 'Teaching the Holocaust with the Use of Active Learning Methods: The Case of a Lower Secondary School with a High Number of Neo-Nazi Supporters in Northern Greece', in *ICERI2013 Proceedings: 6ᵗʰ International Conference of Education, Research and Innovation*, Seville, Spain, November 18–20, 2013, pp. 3758–3764, p. 3758.

DOI: 10.1057/9781137388575.0005

2
Responses to Holocaust Education

Abstract: *There are a number of important factors which determine the myriad ways in which students and teachers respond to Holocaust education. One of the most significant of these is national consciousness and the relationship between a country and its past. In addition to this, responses to Holocaust education are often determined by political and religious attitudes towards Israel and the Jews. In some cases it seems that there is significant opposition to studying the Holocaust, while in other cases students and teachers demonstrate enthusiasm and commitment. The emotional responses to Holocaust education are also evaluated.*

Keywords: assimilation; Israel; national consciousness; Palestine; trauma

Gray, Michael. *Contemporary Debates in Holocaust Education*. Basingstoke: Palgrave Macmillan, 2014. DOI: 10.1057/9781137388575.0006.

In light of its increasing politicisation, in addition to its macabre and harrowing nature, it is unsurprising that the Holocaust often provokes a passionate assortment of intellectual and emotional responses from teachers and students alike. Yet the range of reactions which appear is much more extensive than simply inquisitiveness and grief. Often fused with nationalist agendas, geo-political outlooks and religious persuasions, the teaching of the Holocaust can be greeted with apathy, disrespect or even denial. Explaining why certain responses emerge relies upon understanding a complex tapestry of reasons which often transcend generalisation and are typically dependent upon enquiries at personal, institutional and national level.

The Holocaust and national consciousness

In contrast to many countries in Western Europe, the idea of studying the Holocaust appears to be an unwelcome one to some of the governments and school communities in parts of Central and Eastern Europe. This reluctance to engage with either the associated historical debates or the teaching of the Holocaust is inexorably linked to national histories and contemporary political agendas. Gross and Stevick wrote:

> Today the teaching of the Holocaust is bound up with the histories of the societies in which it is taught; with questions of global politics and power, of religious and ideological perspectives, of guilt, responsibility, and victimhood, with national narratives of heroism and suffering, and of identity itself.[1]

Many post-Soviet states, in what Snyder famously called 'the bloodlands', therefore prefer to place an emphasis on the non-Jewish victims who suffered during the Second World War, including (and perhaps especially) those who were the recipients of Communist as well as Nazi terror. According to Katz, within this region there is a drive to draw comparisons and parallels between the Nazi and Soviet forces.[2] Stevick comments that 'because these campaigns have a political resonance inside the Baltic States, that takes a substantial degree of local knowledge and language ability to track, they are often overlooked or misconstrued by outsiders.'[3] Within much of Central and Eastern Europe, Holocaust education is thus not the Auschwitz-centric approach of its Western neighbours but an often marginalised part of a larger story of national suffering at the hands of Soviet as well as Nazi aggression. This helps

DOI: 10.1057/9781137388575.0006

to avoid highlighting the extent of wartime collaboration and bystander inaction in many of these countries. It must also be taken into account that during the Soviet era, any meaningful discourse or debate on the Holocaust was suppressed and thus it is unsurprising that many teachers continue to work within the parameters of what Frankl calls 'the old frames of reference'.[4]

The antagonistic response to Holocaust education is thus perpetuated by the national and political outlook, which manifests itself in the attitudes and practices of its teachers. In Estonia, for example, the way in which a national day of Holocaust commemoration was to be implemented in schools was purposefully made a free choice by the Ministry of Education when it was introduced in 2003. As it transpired, the day itself was poorly received by most teachers and consequently not implemented.[5] Stevick writes:

> Estonian officials drew upon practices developed under Soviet hegemony that enabled ambiguous communication that would satisfy foreigners that proper commemoration was occurring, even while conveying a different message to Estonian listeners.[6]

Misco's research in Latvia suggested that after regaining independence in 1991, 'teaching about the Holocaust as it occurred in Latvia remained a rarity'.[7] Studies in Moldova suggest a similar picture to many of its neighbours with a focus on national memory and a predominant commemoration of non-Jewish victims. Tartakovsky states that in recent years there has been the establishing 'of a pro-Romanian nationalistic slant in the history curriculum of the national education system'.[8] Moreover, 'perception of Jew as alien communist has remained quite strong in the Moldovan and Romanian national consciousness, perpetuated by a school curriculum that seeks to bolster national pride against a background of historic Romanian suffering and victimisation.'[9]

The issue of national suffering and its centrality within the educational system and the teaching of the Holocaust is perhaps no more acutely felt than in Poland. Complexities in the teaching of the Second World War in Poland are manifold. While their territory was the location of the infamous death camps, millions of Polish citizens were also murdered – Christian Poles as well as Jews. While many of the nation's citizens were bystanders, there are also tales of heroism and valour.

According to Błuszkowski, Poland has 'a solid sense of national separateness'[10] and its historical identity is both 'anachronistic' and

DOI: 10.1057/9781137388575.0006

'ethnocentric'.[11] Milerski describes this as 'endogeneity', whereby, 'people prefer to perceive history, social phenomena, and interpersonal relations from the perspective of an imagined "national interest".'[12] Milerski's empirical research to date on 150 schools in Central Poland would support this. Although many teachers appeared to teach the Holocaust and see it as an important means of forming pupils' moral sensitivities, only 45 per cent 'supported treating the Holocaust in an isolated and special way'.[13] Fifty-one per cent of respondents identified with the notion that one ought to remember that Nazi crimes in Poland 'affected not only Jews, but also the entire population of Poland'.[14]

The somewhat antagonistic response to the study of the Holocaust, which is prevalent in many parts of Central and Eastern Europe, appears to principally stem from a politically motivated reluctance to intellectually engage with the past and a desire to promote and recognise national identities and national suffering. As the generation that lived through the Second World War pass away, and as many Baltic State countries push for closer European integration, the future of Holocaust education in this part of the world perhaps lies in a more pluralistic approach to the past, which recognises the Holocaust as a singular and Jewish tragedy without diminishing the memory or suffering of non-Jewish victims, including the crimes perpetrated by the Soviet Union.

In contrast to demonstrating reluctance over the teaching of the Holocaust, Germany, at both national and local level, has developed a conscientious and contrite Holocaust education. Yet in a similar way to their Eastern neighbours, they too have lodged their curriculum in the contexts of national identity and memory. Gryglewski argues that in Germany the 'predominant educational concept for teaching about the Holocaust' is 'a "national" approach which implies that German pupils need to learn about this history because their parents and grandparents were the ones responsible for the crimes committed'.[15] This narrow pedagogic rationale does not always relate to German youth who are tired of being given a historical diet of guilt or who are first or second generation immigrants whose family history is not even in some tangential way connected to the atrocities of the Holocaust. Avraham notes:

> While for local teachers and students the events of the Holocaust and World War II constituted part of their national history, whether directly or indirectly, for schoolchildren who come from immigrant families (especially from outside Europe) or have immigrant experiences, such history might appear less relevant.[16]

DOI: 10.1057/9781137388575.0006

Gryglewski's solution to this evolving problem is 'appreciation as a teaching method'. This involves a multifaceted approach which includes broadening the scope of Holocaust education. This includes reference to documents which make mention of some of the countries of many of the pupils' families or to highlight 'Nazi racial theories which refer to Asians' or 'Turkish Jews'.[17] Central to the notion of appreciation is also listening to the pupils share their own personal, cultural or ethnic stories and experiences so that they feel included. When this takes place, Gryglewski argues that young people of non-German ethnicity are much more willing to learn about the history of National Socialism.[18]

Association and identification

Yet how do teachers and pupils respond to the Holocaust outside of Europe, when it has less immediate relevance to their national history, memory or identity? Is it possible for those learning about the subject to find resonance with this 'European' chapter of history?

Within America, such resonance has been found by connecting the teaching of the Holocaust to national experiences and problematic social issues such as racism and sexism. Within the United States, 'Facing History and Ourselves' has been at the forefront of Holocaust pedagogy, with its curriculum being used in schools across the country. This programme, which has been the subject of heated scholarly and political debates, has had at its core the desire to change attitudes and approaches towards society. As Riley, Washington and Humphries point out, the creation and subsequent funding (or lack thereof) became inherently linked to liberal/conservative debates and the nature of Holocaust education, as offered by FHAO is more of a sociology programme than a history one:

> While many students who have engaged *Facing History* may come away from the experience with a changed attitude about racism in the United States, they may know little about the history of anti-Semitism and the elements of genocide during the Third Reich.[19]

Yet Polak notes that while 'the study of the Holocaust has gained in importance in the western world during recent decades... [it] is still uncommon in regions such as South America, Africa, Asia and the Middle East'.[20] This slightly crude generalisation is refined by the exceptional work of the USHMM and the Salzburg Global Seminar in their

DOI: 10.1057/9781137388575.0006

very recent publication 'Global Perspectives on Holocaust Education: Trends, Patterns and Practices'. This important document describes the status and nature of Holocaust education in the countries which are not a part of the International Holocaust Remembrance Alliance (IHRA). It outlines some of the complexities and factors which have influenced the official and popular approach to Holocaust education. Nevertheless, this publication does not really explore the responses of teachers or students, but rather the public space (or lack of it) for Holocaust education in these countries.

Other significant work over recent years has been conducted by the Anne Frank House (AFH) which has taken travelling exhibitions around the world, trying to make Holocaust education a truly global, rather than simply Western, phenomenon. Writing on their work with the AFH in Latin America, Chyrikins and Vieyra suggest that the Holocaust and, more specifically, the story of Anne Frank can and has been made relevant to a wide variety of young people in places such as Nicaragua and Guatemala. They particularly note how their work seems to resonate and connect with those who have experienced suffering or prejudice.

> During the first pilot projects in Argentina, Chile and Guatemala, it became clear that teachers and students who visited the exhibitions made their own connections to human rights violations in their own countries as part of a history of collective violence, oppression and dictatorship.[21]

Holocaust education outside of the Western world has often sought to emphasise the relationship between the Holocaust and more recent human rights abuses. The South African Holocaust and Genocide Foundation for example 'believes that if education programmes do not make concrete the connection between the prejudices of the past and the prejudices of the present, the only lesson the Holocaust will teach is that the past was terrible'.[22] On other occasions, comparisons have been made by teachers on training programmes or by students in the classroom without any prompting. Writing about Holocaust education courses for teachers in South Africa, Nates observed, 'as many of the educators learn about the Holocaust and genocide, they start "comparing suffering"'.[23] In their Educational Working Group Paper on the Holocaust and other genocides, the Task Force for International Cooperation, Holocaust Education, Remembrance and Research (ITF) (now the IHRA) stated that 'comparing the suffering of individual victims or victim groups' is neither possible nor legitimate.[24] Moreover it runs the risks of trivialising

DOI: 10.1057/9781137388575.0006

or decontextualising the Holocaust. Yet in reality, preventing such comparisons from being made in post-conflict society is no easy thing.

Holocaust education in the South African experience is particular interesting. Unlike many of its continent's neighbours, it has its own Holocaust and Genocide Foundation with specialist centres in Cape Town, Durban and Johannesburg. Yet South African education is still evolving after the years of apartheid with tensions and feelings still very close to the surface, and recent studies of South African Holocaust education have typically emphasised the wealth of challenges and problems which exist. Peterson, for example, highlights the emotional baggage which many teachers bring with them to the classroom in the wake of having lived in a racial state. Like Gryglewski's methods of encouraging pupils to share their own histories, she suggests that:

> Teachers must have the opportunity outside their classrooms to examine their past and come to an understanding of the value of human rights through that examination. If denied this opportunity, they will be unable to shoulder their responsibility to the learners they teach.[25]

Nates observed that many teachers and pupils wanted the crimes of apartheid to be recognised as genocide while some educators concluded that apartheid was not 'as bad as the Holocaust'.[26] Certainly one of the challenges that exist for Holocaust educators in post-conflict societies is to ensure that appropriate and historically grounded responses emerge rather than unhelpful or problematic ones.

Yet finding out how teachers and students respond to the Holocaust in post-conflict countries is not always easy. In Rwanda, for example, the moratorium on the teaching of history was only lifted in 2010 and, despite educational programmes by various NGOs, there is a shortage of empirical data on the nature of responses to the Holocaust. Nevertheless, the work of Facing History and Ourselves (FHAO) has been instrumental in training Rwandan teachers and they have often done so through a study of the Holocaust. In her paper on the subject, Karen Murphy, the Director of FHAO's International Programmes, stated that teaching Rwandan practitioners about the subject 'provides extraordinary opportunities for teachers to make connections to their own violent past, to develop a vocabulary that allows them to do the work of teaching about their own difficult history'.[27] In Cambodia there have been very few opportunities for a discussion of their own genocide in public education and thus it has also been almost impossible to assess responses to the Holocaust.

DOI: 10.1057/9781137388575.0006

In recent years in Japan, there has been a large emphasis on peace education, although 'for many Japanese the history of the Holocaust has been seen as unrelated to their own history'.[28] Nevertheless, the success of the Holocaust Education Centre in Fukuyama City in Hiroshima and the positive responses it has received from teachers and students suggests that the Holocaust is increasingly being taught and well-received within the Japanese educational system.

For very different reasons, Holocaust education in China must also be viewed in the context of its own suffering. According to Xu:

> Holocaust studies/education becomes a valuable reference for the Chinese, allowing them to re-examine the Nanjing Massacre. Admittedly this is an unspoken purpose of Holocaust studies/education in China: to establish a reference between the Holocaust and the Nanjing Massacre.[29]

This recent embracing of Holocaust education stands in contrast to the more traditional position which essentially ignored the Holocaust in order to focus on the fate of Chinese victims at the hands of the Japanese. Xu also notes that 'Holocaust education obviously brings out more human rights discussions among the Chinese',[30] which, either privately or publicly, potentially leads to critical consideration of their own country and government.

It seems that national histories of suffering and personal experiences of conflict can either strengthen or weaken resonance with Jewish suffering in the Holocaust. While in Central and Eastern Europe – countries which lie at the heart of the geographical location of the killings – the Holocaust creates problems which are not compatible with the contemporary political agendas. Conversely, in countries such as South Africa and many parts of Latin America, which are trying to come to terms with their own recent experiences, the Holocaust, which is typically seen as the paradigmatic genocide, seems to provide a helpful framework of reference.

Politics and religion

What is often less helpful for those involved in Holocaust education is the increasingly typical response of learners to shift a discussion of the Holocaust onto a debate about the Israeli–Palestinian conflict. Recent scholarship around the world has highlighted this problem and many

DOI: 10.1057/9781137388575.0006

pupils have demonstrated strong anti-Israel sentiment which has over-shadowed their willingness to engage (and in some cases sympathise) with the fate of the Jews during the Second World War. Schweber wrote, 'Israel's roles in the Israeli–Palestinian conflict and the Middle East generally matter in terms of Holocaust education, both globally and nationally.'[31]

The ODIHR's major report, *Education on the Holocaust and on Anti-Semitism*, explored some of the obstacles to teaching and learning about the Holocaust and acknowledged the impact of contemporary events in the Middle East. In Austria it was noted that 'even though surveys show a decline in the disposition to express anti-Semitic belief the educational system still has to encourage teachers to confront anti-Semitic behaviour and thought – especially in the context of discussing the crisis in Israel/Palestine.'[32] Moreover, one of the general conclusions of the international study was that 'educators reported recently passive defence mechanisms or active sabotage in the classroom, in part due to the suspicion that a one-sided pro-Israel stance on the Middle East conflict is driving Holocaust education.'[33]

In Holocaust teacher training programmes in South Africa, it has been noted that 'some participants try to shift the focus from the Holocaust to the Middle East'[34] and that 'Israel is viewed with suspicion, and there is both official and popular support for the plight of the Palestinian people.'[35] Conversely, in Short's research on Muslim students in England, he noted that while many Muslim students 'may well be antagonistic to Israel ... they are able and willing to separate that country's conflict with the Palestinians from the fate of the Jews in Nazi-occupied Europe.'[36] In Lange's important study of over 5,000 teachers' experiences and perceptions of teaching the Holocaust in Sweden, he found that 19.2 per cent of teachers thought that the Israeli–Palestinian conflict made teaching about the Holocaust more difficult. By contrast, 20.2 per cent thought it made it easier and 60.6 per cent stated that it made teaching the subject neither more nor less difficult.[37]

Unsurprisingly, the issue of both contemporary and historical relations between Israel and Palestine are particularly sensitive in Holocaust education in Israel itself. Shoham, Shiloah and Kalisman's research suggested that for many Arab teachers in Israel it was difficult to discuss the Holocaust without simultaneously referring to the *Nakba*,[38] which they frequently described as the 'Palestinian Holocaust'.[39] They concluded that in their experience, 'the principal difficulty ... in teaching the Holocaust

DOI: 10.1057/9781137388575.0006

to Arab teachers derives from the Israeli–Palestinian conflict, and from the difficulty of the Arab teachers to distinguish mentally between the *Nakba* and the Holocaust in Europe.'[40] These findings, which were based on a sample of only 35 teachers, suggest serious challenges, especially taking into account that the entire sample was teachers who were willing to attend a Holocaust education programme and thus presumably more predisposed to the subject's legitimacy and importance.

Much of the existing research on the impact of contemporary and historical events in the Middle East on teachers' and students' responses to Holocaust education has been based on very small sample sizes, relied upon anecdotal evidence or simplistic generalisations. Gryglewski and Short discuss what might be considered an example of the last of these concerns by highlighting and rejecting the disposition of some scholars to see all Muslim students as a monolithic entity. The former observed, for example, on the basis of his experiences that 'students with a Turkish background, on the whole, did not mention the Israeli–Palestinian conflict. In contrast, mixed groups with students of both Turkish and Palestinian/Arab origin manifested a sense of solidarity and did tend to mention the conflict.'[41] Both Gryglewski and Short in their studies in Germany and England respectively also came to very similar conclusions. Gryglewski noted that 'young people from these backgrounds [Turkish and Arab–Palestinian] do not reject learning about the Holocaust: on the contrary',[42] while Short stated, 'many Muslim students have no objection to learning about the Holocaust and seem as likely as any other group of students to benefit from their learning.'[43] Similar conclusions were drawn by Carr in a study of 21 Muslim students in a school in Cairo, who found no evidence of reluctance.[44] In addition to being incredibly small, Carr's sample could hardly be less representative. Based upon research in one English-speaking international school, too much weight ought not to be placed on the findings.

Somewhat hypocritically, Short describes Rutland's valuable qualitative study of Muslim pupils' responses to the Holocaust in Australia as 'extremely small-scale'[45] while he himself also had a sample size of 15. While Short interviewed the head of history in 15 schools which had a Muslim student majority, Rutland interviewed both high school teachers and educational facilitators. She concluded that in schools with large Muslim populations in Sydney, there was virulent and violent anti-Semitism, characterised by death threats to Jews, admiration for the

DOI: 10.1057/9781137388575.0006

Nazis and disappointment that the Holocaust had not gone 'far enough'.[46] Evidence also suggested that:

> The students are exposed to anti-Jewish beliefs at home, in their local mosques, and in material sold in Muslim bookshops... [They] experience a sense of disconnection when their teachers tell them something different about the Jewish people or the Holocaust from what they have learnt at home.[47]

If the experiences which Rutland describes are characteristic, either of some Muslim students in Australia or of some Muslim students more generally, then this poses a very serious problem for Holocaust educators. Serious attention needs to be given on how to deconstruct and tackle prejudicial attitudes against Jews. This may involve finding successful ways of challenging the alternative Holocaust education which some young Muslims are being exposed to within the local mosque or within their family home.

A more nuanced look at Short's work in England suggests some support for Rutland's findings in Australia. Within some schools in his study, for example, 'negative stereotyping of Jews was said to be endemic',[48] while another said of teaching Muslim students:

> It's quite difficult because they think Hitler was great and everything he did was great and they will occasionally just come out with comments like 'it's a pity he didn't finish it off' and 'yes [the Holocaust] was a good thing because [the Jews] weren't really German were they and they were only doing things for themselves'.[49]

Moreover, a report carried out on behalf of the French government in 2010 showed that Muslim students frequently expressed anti-Semitic views during lessons on the Holocaust, with some of them using inappropriate 'humour' and refusing to watch certain films on the subject.[50] One of the most valuable studies on Muslim students' responses to the Holocaust was carried out by Jikeli who conducted 117 face-to-face interviews with young male Muslims in London, Berlin and Paris between 2005 and 2007. He found that the majority of those interviewed condemned the Holocaust and found empathy with the Jewish victims. Nevertheless, Jikeli argued that Muslim's views about the Holocaust are shaped by their attitudes towards the Jews.

> Antisemitic views shape distorted views of the Holocaust such as diminishing the Holocaust, inappropriate comparisons or outright Holocaust denial or even the approval of the Holocaust... Equations of Jews with Nazis or

DOI: 10.1057/9781137388575.0006

Palestinians today with Jews in the past are motivated by antisemitism and shaped by a Manichean view of the Israeli–Palestinian conflict, not by a lack of knowledge.[51]

The HEDP report in England also noted that:

The teacher who remarked that 'even in a school that is 70% Muslim ... I take a historical disciplinary perspective' indicates a problematic and growing perception that students from specific national/religious backgrounds are resistant to learning about the Holocaust.[52]

It appears that despite some work in this particular field, there is considerable need for further studies which employ larger sample sizes and engage in more systematic research with more sophisticated analysis. These must explore Muslim youths from different backgrounds, different ethnic origins and who have been exposed to different influences.

Making connections between the Holocaust and the creation of the State of Israel seems common therefore among many Muslim youths, despite the fact that many educators seem to try to minimise the relationship. Nevertheless, there is evidence to suggest that within many Jewish schools the historical links between the two are cultivated and fostered. In her compelling article on Diasporic Zionism and Jewish Holocaust education, Silverstein found that 12 out of 15 teachers explicitly linked the end of the Holocaust with the creation of the State of Israel.[53]

Whether teachers in interviews consciously described the creation of Israel as the redemptive national end to the Holocaust, or followed a Zionist narratorial path of teaching Israel's creation after the unit on the Holocaust, we can understand that Israel is a constant, redemptive, and masculinist presence in these teachings.[54]

Silverstein's research was carried out in seven Jewish schools in New York and in five Jewish schools in Melbourne. Through the structure of their curricula and the nature of their teaching, many teachers within these institutions present the Declaration of Independence as the 'happy ending' to the Holocaust.

In Schweber's qualitative study of Holocaust education in a Lubavitch girls' Yeshivah, she also observed the impact of Israel on the way that the course was taught. Not only were analogies frequently made between historical references and contemporary Israel to aid understanding, but 'the girls' predisposition to identify with European Jews and with current day Israelis was reified and strengthened'.[55]

DOI: 10.1057/9781137388575.0006

Teachers' and pupils' responses to the Holocaust, especially among Muslims and Jews, do appear to be affected and influenced by their understanding and interpretation of the events in the Middle East and specifically by their views on the State of Israel. Whether or not educators choose to deal with issues relating to the Israeli–Palestinian conflict is an important question. For many, the frequency with which students mention it means that the subject can hardly be avoided. How they deal with it is a different question altogether. Arguably, teachers should teach about it as part of their study of the Holocaust for as Bauer suggests,

> Although the Holocaust itself occurred during the world war, the *period* of the Holocaust stretches from the rise of the Nazi regime in 1933 to the dissolution of the displaced person camps in Central Europe after the war. In these camps the core of the survivors lived until 1948.[56]

Emotional responses and affective learning

While political and religious views can undoubtedly lead to emotional responses to the Holocaust, it seems this can also be the case among those teachers and students who approach the subject from a less partisan perspective. The very subject matters of the Holocaust, principally death, destruction and annihilation, have the potential to generate a plethora of powerful and compelling feelings from both those who teach it and are taught about it. Richardson sagaciously commented:

> That the Holocaust is a topic laden with emotion is self-evident. But what that emotion might be – and how someone encountering the Holocaust might deal with it – is far more complex and difficult to foresee, particularly where young people are involved. Some learners might experience shock, others guilt, vulnerability, sadness, titillation or defensiveness and different students will emotionally engage with different things.[57]

Within Holocaust education, this has led to important debates about the appropriate age when children ought to study the topic at school, famously characterised by the divergence of Sepinwall[58] and Totten.[59] In his article, 'Should there be Holocaust Education for K–4 Students? The Answer is No', Totten convincingly argues that the history of the Holocaust is far too complex for young children to understand. Moreover, he asserts that children ought not to be exposed to the subject and its distressing subject matter if they are incapable of understanding it. Despite this set of arguments, increasingly younger children are being introduced to the

DOI: 10.1057/9781137388575.0006

Holocaust, which Totten would prefer to call 'Pre-Holocaust Education' or 'preparatory Holocaust Education'.

This particular debate was helped no end by the valuable and thoughtful contribution of Schweber's 2008 article '"What Happened to Their Pets?": Third Graders Encounter the Holocaust', which highlighted the increasing creep of the Holocaust into the curriculum. This qualitative study of 24 eight and nine-year-olds convincingly demonstrated that pupils fell into one of two categories. Either they understood the subject matter and became depressed or they failed to understand; options which Schweber describes as a situation which 'poses "no wins".'[60] In this ethnographic study, the teacher gradually exposed the children to the nature and extent of the Nazis' crimes, including showing them pictures of corpses and mass graves. Individual pupils were described as 'confused and upset',[61] 'upset and shocked'[62] with another stating, 'I just got so scared, mad and sad, all at the same time... It's painful to think about.'[63] The experiences of this final pupil were particularly elaborated on in Schweber's findings. She was an intelligent Jewish girl who grasped more than her peers and often struggled to deal with their immature emotional responses and childlike comments. As a direct result of her study of the Holocaust, this girl had suffered depression, visited the school counsellor and endured nightmares. Her mother observed that her daughter had become morose, quiet, losing interest in things and had experienced 'a real depression'.[64] One-fifth of the other students also experienced nightmares.[65] Studies on the emotional impact of Holocaust education raise serious ethical issues and researchers need to take great care that their studies don't exacerbate the situation. In Schweber's research, for example, the Jewish girl referred to above could not complete her post-course interview as she was too 'emotionally raw to re-visit the Holocaust'.[66]

Jennings's work, also conducted in America, exhibits emotional responses being demonstrated by pupils who studied the Holocaust – in this instance among ten and eleven-year-olds.[67] In an ethnographic study of 520 bilingual students who learnt about the subject as part of a citizenship programme about tolerance, respondents appeared emotionally affected and sympathetic. Yet such responses were in many senses an inevitable product of the sort of Holocaust programme which was being taught. It seems that the principal aim was not to enable the children to acquire a contextualised or historical knowledge and understanding of the subject but to engage them emotionally. It thus appears unsurprising that young children were sensitised when they were asked to write letters to Anne Frank and identify with children who were murdered. Such tactics seem somewhat sensationalist with dubious long-term pedagogic benefits.

In the United Kingdom, the Nottinghamshire-based Holocaust Centre has a permanent exhibition specifically aimed for pupils aged 11 years or younger. It enables visitors to explore the lives of children who survived the Holocaust and exposes them to themes such as anti-Semitism, *Kristallnacht* and the *Kindertransport*. Bhana observed in her experiences of this exhibition that pupils were 'mature and wholly engaged',[68] concluding that 'learning about the Holocaust is accessible and can be appropriate for primary aged children'.[69] Yet despite Bhana's position on the issue, the experience did affect pupils. One child wrote concerning his visit and meeting of a survivor that 'it was really emotional to hear her story but the experience made the Holocaust feel more real than it was in the classroom.'[70]

Viewing artefacts, meeting survivors and visiting sites can, it would seem, be more of an emotional experience than learning about the subject in the classroom. In an evaluation by Cowan and Maitles of students visiting Auschwitz from schools in Scotland, one pupil commented, 'I was physically sick because of the emotion.'[71] Another noted, 'I couldn't take in what I was seeing. I was fine when I first came home, but then days after, it played with my head.'[72] Bastel, Mtzka and Miklas carried out an empirical study of how 60 13–15-year-olds from a private school in Vienna responded when visiting Mauthausen concentration camp in Austria. They observed that around a quarter of the pupils showed emotional concern and 'about 50% were horrified at the large number of people killed, and also at the cruelty people can show'.[73] In addition, Clyde noted some very demonstrative and affective reactions which were expressed by 18–25 year olds after their educational visit to Poland on 'The March of Remembrance and Hope' programme. One participant wrote:

> Auschwitz/Birkenau and Majdanek will never be forgotten. I still have nightmares; I can still smell Auschwitz as I write this response. I have never been filled with as much despair viewing Birkenau, or as much rage viewing Majdanek.[74]

Another response stated, 'our trip to Majdanek changed my life forever. I can't even talk about that component of our trip without crying... As hard as it was to be there, I'm glad we went.'[75] Conversely one could argue

DOI: 10.1057/9781137388575.0006

that such emotive responses were not necessarily typical seeing that only 78 out of a possible 268 participants replied to the follow-up research. Nevertheless, it seems that Holocaust education, both within the classroom and perhaps especially outside of it, has the potential to produce emotive and powerful reactions, irrespective of the age of the individual.

In his doctoral research on the types of learning that take place when students encounter the Holocaust, Richardson also found that 'learning about the Holocaust had been an emotionally traumatic and complicated process'.[76] His study of 48 students in one English school between the ages of 13 and 18 generated a wide variety of responses ranging from cognitive dissonance to greater self-reflection.[77] The 2009 study of over 2000 teachers in England by the HEDP provided a much more methodologically robust range of responses which have been experienced in the classroom. While some teachers worried that their teaching sometimes traumatised their pupils, others expressed 'anger, frustration or disappointment at what was, from their perspective, students' "inappropriate" responses. Some worried that their students were becoming "anaesthetised" to violence'.[78] Others mentioned that they themselves often became upset and that teaching it involved 'emotional discomfort and pain' with one teacher suggesting that 'the biggest challenge she faced was "not crying" in front of students'.[79] Hondius too observed that 'teachers themselves have rarely come to terms with the events emotionally (as well as the students and parents)'.[80] This is characterised by the comments of Blutinger, who suggests that the affective impact of the Holocaust is an important part of teaching this emotive subject.

> I tell my students the first day of class that not only should they feel comfortable crying, but that I may cry as well from time to time. While part of me wishes that I could just become inured to this material, I also know that if I did so, I would no longer really be engaged with the subject. The pain is an occupational hazard of teaching this sort of history.[81]

In an attempt to deal with the emotional impact of teaching the Holocaust, the Israel Center for the Treatment of Pyschotrauma in Jerusalem 'are now beginning to offer courses addressing the emotional impact of being a Shoah educator'.[82]

Writing principally about Holocaust education in the United Kingdom, Epstein castigated the lack of research into trauma and the emotional impact of Holocaust education and children's literature, without any seeming awareness of the existing scholarly corpus.

DOI: 10.1057/9781137388575.0006

There has not even been much research into issues such as at what age or level of maturity children can handle learning about the Holocaust, how to teach them about it, or whether trauma/pain could in fact be necessary.[83]

Her article provoked strong responses from Andrews, Gray and Maws who each challenged different areas of her premise and critiqued her generalisations, inaccuracies and simplifications.[84]

It seems therefore that teaching and learning about the Holocaust does provoke emotional responses and a wide variety of them. Van Driel and Van Dijk note that 'the emotions (and sometimes trauma) that discussion of the Holocaust can unleash create a challenge for educators.'[85] Clearly selecting the right age and appropriate methodology is of the utmost importance and goes at least some way in dealing with these challenges. Yet this is a complex area and the various empirical studies to date offer no easy or simple answers. Moreover, there remains no consensus on aims (emotionally or intellectually) among Holocaust educators around the world and what sort of responses ought to be encouraged from learners. Should educators be trying to arouse an emotional response or avoid one? Is the Holocaust simply being used as a tool to connect people's understanding to their own human rights abuses, which may be more personally distressing, and is this an appropriate use of the Holocaust? These questions are all connected to the emotional responses of those learning about the Holocaust.

Other responses

Holocaust education has produced other responses, many of which necessitate further empirical research. Schweber has noted that the frequency of teaching this subject can cause 'Holocaust fatigue' with one teacher commenting, 'my kids are sick of it, sick of the Holocaust'.[86] A report on Holocaust education in Italy stated that 'overdose of information may cause boredom and even latent hostility'.[87] Controversial reactions to the Holocaust however, are not always necessarily about the Holocaust per se. Many students know that reverence and deference are popularly attached to the subject and thus rebellious behaviour is perceived to be more 'extreme' when applied to it.

Overall it seems that Holocaust education provokes and produces a wide range of responses from governments and institutions to teachers and students. Many of these reactions pose challenges and dilemmas for the field, which do not appear to have any immediate or easy solutions.

DOI: 10.1057/9781137388575.0006

Notes

1   Gross, Z. and Stevick E. D. (2010) 'Holocaust Education – International Perspectives: Challenges, Opportunities and Research', *Prospects*, 40: 1, 17–33, p. 22.

2   Katz, D. (2009) 'On Three Definitions: Genocide, Holocaust Denial, Holocaust Obfuscation', in Donskis, L. (Ed.) *A Litmus Test Case of Modernity: Examining Modern Sensibilities and the Public Domain in the Baltic States at the Turn of the Century*, (Bern: Peter Lang), 259–277.

3   Stevick, D. (2012) 'The Holocaust in the Contemporary Baltic States: International Relations, Politics, and Education, Holocaust', *Study and Research*, (Holocaust: Studii și cercetări), 1: 5, 87–103, p. 100.

4   Frankl, M. (2003) 'Holocaust Education in the Czech Republic, 1989–2002', *Intercultural Education*, 14: 2, 177–189, p. 178.

5   Stevick, 'The Holocaust in the Contemporary Baltic States', p. 95.

6   Stevick, 'The Holocaust in the Contemporary Baltic States', p. 95.

7   Misco, T. (2007) 'Holocaust Curriculum Development for Latvian Schools: Arriving at Purposes, Aims, and Goals through Curriculum Deliberation', *Theory and Research in Social Education*, 35: 3, 393–426, p. 394.

8   Tartakovsky, D. (2008) 'Conflicting Holocaust Narratives in Moldovan Nationalist Historical Discourse', *East European Jewish Affairs*, 38: 2, 211–229, p. 212.

9   Tartakovsky, 'Conflicting Holocaust Narratives', p. 215.

10 Błuszkowski, J. (2005) *Stereotypy a to Zsamos´c´ Narodowa* [Stereotypes and National Identity], (Warsaw: Dom Wydawniczy Elipsa), p. 144.

11 Błuszkowski, *Stereotypy a to Zsamos´c´ Narodowa*, p. 147.

12 Milerski, B. (2010) 'Holocaust Education in Polish Public Schools: Between Remembrance and Civic Education', *Prospects*, 40: 1, 115–132, p. 117.

13 Milerski, 'Holocaust Education in Polish Public Schools', p. 129.

14 Milerski, 'Holocaust Education in Polish Public Schools', p. 129.

15 Gryglewski, E. (2010) 'Teaching about the Holocaust in Multicultural Societies: Appreciating the Learner', *Intercultural Education*, 21: S1, S41–S49, p. S41.

16 Avraham, D. (2010) 'The Problem with using Historical Parallels as a Method in Holocaust and Genocide Teaching', *Intercultural Education*, 21: S1, S33–S40, p. S33.

17 Avraham, 'The Problem with using Historical Parallels', p. S44.

18 Avraham, 'The Problem with using Historical Parallels', p. S44.

19 Riley, K., Washington, E. and Humphries, E. (2011) 'Facing History and Ourselves: Noble Purpose, Unending Controversy', in Totten, S. and Pedersen, J. (Eds) *Teaching and Studying Social Issues: Major Programs and Approaches*, (Charlotte, North Carolina: Information Age Publishing), pp. 119–139, p. 135.

DOI: 10.1057/9781137388575.0006

20 Polak, K. (2010) 'Tolerance Education in Morocco. "Anne Frank: A History for Today": Learning about our Past – Contributing to our Future', *Intercultural Education*, 21: S1, S51–S59, p. S51.

21 Chyrikins, M. and Vieyra, M. (2010) 'Making the Past Relevant to Future Generations. The Work of the Anne Frank House in Latin America', *Intercultural Education*, 21: S1, S7–S15, p. S11.

22 Peterson, T. (2010) 'Moving beyond the Toolbox: Teaching Human Rights through Teaching the Holocaust in Post-Apartheid South Africa', *Intercultural Education*, 21, S1, S27–S31, p. S28.

23 Nates, T. (2010) ' "But, Apartheid was also Genocide... What about our suffering?" Teaching the Holocaust in South Africa – Opportunities and Challenges', *Intercultural Education*, 21: S1, S17–S26, p. S22.

24 Task Force for International Cooperation, Holocaust Education, Remembrance and Research. (2010) 'Educational Working Group Paper on the Holocaust and other Genocides', p. 5.

25 Peterson, 'Moving beyond the Toolbox', p. S30.

26 Nates, 'But, Apartheid was also Genocide', p. S22.

27 Murphy, K. (2010) 'Example of Best Practice 1. Teaching a Holocaust Case Study in a Post-Conflict Environment: Education as Part of Violence, Reconstruction and Repair', *Intercultural Education*, 21: S1, S71–S77, p. S76.

28 Otsuka, M. (1999) 'Importance of Holocaust Education in Japan', *Journal of Genocide Research*, 1: 3, 459–462, p. 459.

29 Xu, X. (2009) 'Holocaust Education in China', *The Holocaust and the United Nations Outreach Programme Discussion Papers Journal*, (New York: United Nations), pp. 15–16.

30 Xu 'Holocaust Education in China', p. 16.

31 Schweber, S. (2006) 'Holocaust Fatigue', *Social Education*, 7: 1, 44–50, p. 51.

32 Office for Democratic Institutions and Human Rights. (2005) *Education on the Holocaust and on Anti-Semitism*, p. 38.

33 ODIHR, *Education on the Holocaust*, p. 132.

34 Nates, 'But, Apartheid was also Genocide', p. S24

35 Nates, 'But, Apartheid was also Genocide', p. S24.

36 Short, G. (2013) 'Reluctant Learners? Muslim Youth Confront the Holocaust', *Intercultural Education*, 24: 1–2, 121–132, 128–129.

37 Lange, A. (2008) *A Survey of Teachers' Experiences and Perceptions in Relation to Teaching about the Holocaust* (Stockholm: Living History Forum), p. 62.

38 'Nakba' mean 'catastrophe' and is the term used by Palestinians to describe the displacement of persons relating to the Israeli Declaration of Independence.

39 Shoham, E., Shiloah, N. and Kalisman, R. (2003) 'Arab Teachers and Holocaust Education: Arab Teachers Study Holocaust Education in Israel', *Teaching and Teacher Education*, 19, 609–625, p. 617.

DOI: 10.1057/9781137388575.0006

40   Shoham et al., 'Arab Teachers', p. 623.

41   Gryglewski, 'Teaching about the Holocaust', p. S44.

42   Gryglewski, 'Teaching about the Holocaust', p. S44.

43   Short, 'Reluctant learners?', pp. 128–129.

44   Carr, H. (2012) *How do Children in an Egyptian International School Respond to the Teaching of the Holocaust?* Unpublished MEd thesis, University of Hull.

45   Short, 'Reluctant Learners?', p. 127.

46   Rutland, S. (2010) 'Creating Effective Holocaust Education Programmes for Government Schools with Large Muslim Populations in Sydney', *Prospects* 40: 1, 75–91, p. 81.

47   Rutland, 'Creating Effective', p. 82.

48   Short, 'Reluctant Learners?', p. 125.

49   Short, 'Reluctant Learners?', p. 126.

50   Haut Conseil à l'intégration, *Les défis de l'intégration à l'école, pp. 93–95.*

51   Jikeli, G. (2013) 'Perceptions of the Holocaust among Young Muslims in Berlin, Paris and London', in Jikeli, G. and Allouche-Benayoun, J. (Eds) *Perceptions of the Holocaust in Europe and Muslim Communities, Muslims in Global Societies Series,* (New York: Springer), 105–131, pp. 105–106.

52   Pettigrew, A., Foster, S., Howson, J., Salmons, P., Lenga, R- A. and Andrews, K. (2009) *Teaching about the Holocaust in English Secondary Schools: An Empirical Study of National Trends, Perspectives and Practice,* (Holocaust Education Development Programme, Institute of Education, University of London), p. 89.

53   Silverstein, J. (2012) ' "From the Utter Depth of Degradation to the Apogee of Bliss": The Genderings of Diasporic Zionism and Jewish Holocaust Education', *Journal of Modern Jewish Studies*, 11: 3, 377–398, p. 383.

54   Silverstein, 'From the Utter Depth', p. 383.

55   Schweber, S. (2008) ' "Here There Is No Why": Holocaust Education at a Lubavitch Girls' Yeshivah', *Jewish Social Studies*, 14: 2, 156–185, p. 177.

56   Bauer, Y. (2001) *Re-thinking the Holocaust*, (New Haven: Yale University Press), p. 242.

57   Richardson, A. (2012) *Holocaust Education: An Investigation into the Types of Learning That Take Place When Students Encounter the Holocaust.* Unpublished EdD Thesis, Brunel University, p. 114.

58   Sepinwall, H. (1999) 'Incorporating Holocaust Education into K–4 Curriculum and Teaching in the United States', *Social Studies and the Young Learner*, 10: 3, 5–8.

59   Totten, S. (1999) 'Should There Be Holocaust Education for K–4 Students? The Answer is No', *Social Sciences and the Young Learner*, 12: 1, 36–39.

60   Schweber, S. (2008) ' "What Happened to Their Pets?": Third Graders Encounter the Holocaust', *Teachers College Record*, 110: 10, 2073–2115, p. 2080.

61   Schweber, 'What Happened to Their Pets?', p. 2088.

DOI: 10.1057/9781137388575.0006

62   Schweber, 'What Happened to Their Pets?', p. 2090.

63   Schweber, 'What Happened to Their Pets?', p. 2102.

64   Schweber, 'What Happened to Their Pets?', p. 2104.

65   Schweber, 'What Happened to Their Pets?', p. 2105.

66   Schweber, 'What Happened to Their Pets?', p. 2108.

67   Jennings, L. (2010) 'Challenges and Possibilities of Holocaust Education and Critical Citizenship: An Ethnographic Study of a Fifth-Grade Bilingual Class Revisited', *Prospects*, 40: 1, 35–56.

68   Bhana, K. (2012) 'Case Study 5: Is Teaching about the Holocaust suitable for Primary Aged Children?', *Primary History*, Summer, 29–30, p. 30.

69   Bhana, 'Case Study 5', p. 30.

70   Bhana, 'Case Study 5', p. 30.

71   Cowan, P. and Maitles, H. (2011) ' "We saw Inhumanity Close Up". What Is Gained by School Students from Scotland Visiting Auschwitz?', *Journal of Curriculum Studies*, 43: 2, 163–184, p. 174.

72   Cowan, and Maitles, 'We saw Inhumanity Close Up', p. 176.

73   Bastel, H., Mtzka, C. and Miklas, H. (2010) 'Holocaust Education in Austria: A (Hi)story of Complexity and Ambivalence', *Prospects*, 40: 1, 57–73, p. 69.

74   Clyde, C. (2010) 'Developing Civic Leaders through an Experiential Learning Programme for Holocaust Education', *Prospects*, 40: 2, 289–306, p. 301.

75   Clyde, 'Developing Civic Leaders', p. 301.

76   Richardson, *Holocaust Education*, p. 2.

77   Richardson, *Holocaust Education*, p. 112.

78   Pettigrew et al., *Teaching about the Holocaust*, pp. 91–92.

79   Pettigrew et al., *Teaching about the Holocaust*, p. 91.

80   Hondius, D. (2010) 'Finding Common Good in Education about the Holocaust and Slavery', *Intercultural Education*, 21: S1, S61–S69, p. S62.

81   Blutinger, 'Bearing Witness', p. 277.

82   Cohen, E. (2013) *Identity and Pedagogy: Shoah Education in Israeli State Schools*, (Brighton, MA: Academic Studies Press), p. 98.

83   Epstein, B. J. (2013) 'Inflicting Trauma: The Ethics of Writing and Teaching the Holocaust for Children', *Holocaust Studies: A Journal of Culture and History*, 19: 1, 101–120, p. 115.

84   Andrews, K., Gray, M. and Maws, A. (2013) 'Responses to BJ Epstein's "Inflicting Trauma" ', *Holocaust Studies: A Journal of Culture and History*, 19: 1, 121–134.

85   Van Driel, B. and Van Dijk, L. (2010) 'Diverse Classrooms – Opportunities and Challenges', *Intercultural Education*, 21: S1, S1–S5, p. S2.

86   Schweber, S. (2006) 'Holocaust Fatigue', *Social Education*, 7: 1, 44–50, p. 50.

87   ODIHR, *Education on the Holocaust*, p. 37.

DOI: 10.1057/9781137388575.0006

3
The Quality of Research and Scholarship

Abstract: *This chapter critically scrutinises the standards of scholarship within the field of Holocaust education by analysing research design, sample size and composition, as well as objectivity. While acknowledging certain studies which employ robust methodologies, the quality of much of the work within the field is called into question. In addition, the key areas within Holocaust education which have largely been marginalised or ignored are highlighted, demonstrating areas where future researchers may wish to focus their efforts.*

Keywords: design; methodology; research; sample; validity

Gray, Michael. *Contemporary Debates in Holocaust Education*. Basingstoke: Palgrave Macmillan, 2014. DOI: 10.1057/9781137388575.0007.

DOI: 10.1057/9781137388575.0007

Within every discipline, be it medicine, quantum physics or the social sciences, there are means of assessing the quality of research which may vary according to the nature of the field, but nevertheless principally revolve around methodological issues. When such scrutiny and examination is applied to the scholarship of Holocaust education, it has at times appeared to lack the requisite rigour, robustness and reliability.

Samples

Many of the studies within Holocaust education have naturally revolved around teacher or student participants. Central to the credibility of such studies is the sample; how it was chosen, its size and its composition. If the reader is to trust the findings and conclusions which the author makes, then they need to have confidence in the means whereby they were acquired. This involves the researcher explaining the methodology and demonstrating that the sample which was used was chosen fairly and that it was representative of the broader population. Unless the construction of the sample is methodologically robust, the ability to generalise and hypothesise about the population should rightly be called into question.

Within a number of research papers in Holocaust education, which have often appeared in high quality peer-reviewed journals, the findings have been based on anecdotal evidence, without mention of how the author arrived at these conclusions. Symptomatic of this is a paper by Chyrikins and Vieyra on the work of the Anne Frank House in Latin America. In addition to making vague and relatively meaningless claims such as their work 'shows that the history of the Holocaust can be a very useful educational tool',[1] they also make bold statements about how the diary of Anne Frank serves as a 'source of inspiration ... for those who have experienced oppression' and that their work has contributed to young people gaining 'self-esteem and confidence'.[2] Despite providing no real evidence to support their claims, they suggest that their insights 'can help educators to develop future programmes'.[3]

Moreover, in her work on South African Holocaust education, Nates highlights some interesting challenges and opportunities but bases them upon her experiences of running teacher training programmes and working for the South African Holocaust and Genocide Foundation. While few would doubt that Nates is well placed to comment on Holocaust

DOI: 10.1057/9781137388575.0007

education in South Africa, doing so on the basis of her experiences is not sufficiently credible. The same is true of Chyrikins and Vieyra's work in Latin America. How many teachers and students have participated in the respective programmes? Do they represent a sufficiently diverse cross section of the populations, for example the South African teacher population which Nates records as being 390,000 or the two million South African Muslim population? Moreover, when Nates records that due to events in the Middle East 'the teaching of the Holocaust is at times viewed with suspicion', she is unhelpfully vague about the extent of this suspicion.[4] Had she employed a specific methodology, selected a representative sample and produced quantifiable data on the basis of codifying her comments, then the reader would be much better informed.

This is not to say that the only valuable studies are those with large, diverse samples which produce quantitative results. Schweber's qualitative ethnography of 24 third graders' encounter with the Holocaust is one of the most significant and helpful contributions to the field in recent years[5] and provides a detailed and transparent account of her methodology. She explains the system she employed to codify her transcripts and readily acknowledges that in any 'statistical sense' the study in not generalisable. This critical and reflective approach is often lacking within the scholarship of Holocaust education, with many of those who publish their ideas not coming from a background which is grounded in research training and academia.

Yet even many of those who have outlined their methodology, to a greater or lesser extent, have relied upon a very small and unrepresentative sample. The research of Edwards and O'Dowd, for example, was conducted on only 26 pupils from one school, all of whom were boys.[6] Incidentally, this particular study ought to also be commended for being possibly the very first published empirical study on pupils' preconceptions of the Holocaust in England. The fact remains, however, that a sample size ought to provide confidence in the findings. When the number of interviewees is as small as 15, as in the cases of Rutland and Short's respective works on teaching Muslim students, there must be some reservation when evaluating the usefulness of their findings.[7]

In contrast to the above, it is important to acknowledge that many studies in Holocaust education have been conducted using very sizeable and carefully constructed samples. Cohen, for example, interviewed 307 principles, 519 teachers and 2540 students from a very demographically diverse range of religious and non-religious backgrounds. Moreover,

DOI: 10.1057/9781137388575.0007

in the early 1990s, a survey of young people's associations with the name 'Adolf Hitler' was conducted on nearly 32,000 students in over 25 countries.[8]

Research design

Conducting a reliable study is not solely dependent on the sample. Some recent research in Holocaust education has employed thorough sampling techniques but utilised a flawed instrument. This has been characteristic of some of the surveys conducted by the AJC such as *The Holocaust and Its Implications: A Seven Nation Comparative Study.* Despite interviewing approximately a thousand people in each of the seven countries, as well as stratifying the sample by region and community type, the study contained ambiguous and confusing questions. The worst of these was 'from what you know or have heard, what were Auschwitz, Dachau, and Treblinka?' The options provided were 'concentration camps', 'death camps', 'extermination camps', 'camps', 'other' and 'don't know'. The results from this question are of minimal value because while Treblinka was a death camp and Dachau a concentration camp (both of which are thus also 'camps'), Auschwitz was the term for various camps, including Birkenau and Auschwitz III-Monowitz.

Using closed-ended questions with a list of options can be a problematic way of assessing attitudes and knowledge of the Holocaust, although it appears to have been used in the majority of studies to date. De Vaus writes, 'a major problem of forced-choice questions is that on some issues they can create false opinions either by giving an insufficient range of alternatives from which to choose or by prompting people with acceptable answers.'[9] In addition to that, it gives the opportunity for the respondent to guess correctly, which is then interpreted by the researcher as knowledge. In her insightful article 'Method and Meaning in Holocaust-Knowledge Surveys', Bischoping is critical of closed, multiple-choice questions which 'do not assess critical thinking skills' and limit 'the definition of knowledge to rote memorization.'[10] She also remarks that 'researchers need to make informed decisions about which ways of defining and measuring knowledge yield the most meaningful results.'[11] Despite giving this warning over 15 years ago, it seems that recent scholarship has not heeded it. Even some of the leading research in the field, such as the studies by Lange in Sweden and the HEDP in

DOI: 10.1057/9781137388575.0007

England, assessed teachers' knowledge by asking specific, predominantly closed-ended questions. While there is some value in knowing what respondents don't know, open-ended questions not only demonstrate more effectively what they do know, but provide a richer form of data for analysing what they don't.

The potential danger of using multiple-choice questions is that the choice of options artificially creates answers which would probably not emerge from open-ended ones. This can lead to sensational headlines which mislead the public about the state of Holocaust knowledge. In 2009, for example, to mark the release of *The Boy in the Striped Pyjamas*, Miramax and the London Jewish Cultural Centre commissioned a survey of 1,200 pupils aged 11–16 to test their knowledge of the Holocaust. The results concluded that 2 per cent of respondents thought Auschwitz was a beer and 1 per cent thought it a type of bread.[12] The media were quick to report that some British children thought Auschwitz was a beer, and suggested that if this was nationally representative it was the equivalent of 90,000 students holding this view.

The importance of the wording in a question was especially highlighted in an AJC commissioned survey in 1992.[13] According to their findings 22 per cent of Americans thought it possible the Holocaust never happened in response to a complex question which employed double negatives.[14] When the question was rephrased in 1994[15] the results found that only 1 per cent of Americans thought it possible the Holocaust never happened.[16]

Problematic assumptions

As in any field, research within Holocaust education has been built upon the findings and conclusions which have previously been agreed and established. While this is undoubtedly necessary if knowledge is to advance, it is also highly problematic if studies are built upon intellectual foundations which are questionable. Within the social sciences, and thus within Holocaust education, the nature of knowledge is *a posteriori*, that is, it is not self-justifying. There must thus be compelling evidence to support the intellectual and pedagogic assumptions which underpin research, educational programmes, curricula and exhibitions. Perhaps one of the biggest criticisms of Holocaust education, both in scholarly and practical terms, is that its value to transform, improve and moralise

DOI: 10.1057/9781137388575.0007

its receivers has sometimes been seen as *a priori*, a form of knowledge which is acquired through reason and rationality rather than through empirical research. While there have been a wide range of scholars who have argued against the idea that the Holocaust has 'lessons' for today, such as Kinloch,[17] Novick[18] and Eckmann,[19] a significant number of scholars have either designed their research assuming that it is true or their research has been grounded upon educational programmes which have been based on this assumption. While there have been many valuable papers both of a theoretical and empirical nature by the likes of Short,[20] Cowan, Maitles[21] and others, which support the idea that Holocaust education can moralise the learner, these have not been sufficiently compelling to abandon an alternative position. This is not to say that the Holocaust either does or does not provide lessons – in many senses the debate is far more complex than this dichotomy – but it is to say that there is at present insufficient evidence to justify turning the assumption that it does provide contemporary lessons into the intellectual foundations of scholarship.

Building upon the idea that the Holocaust moralises the learner is demonstrated in Peterson's work on Holocaust and human rights education with the South African Holocaust and Genocide Foundation. She acknowledges, with some caveats, that 'the first assumption is that learning about past human rights abuses will automatically affect the present and thus the future in a positive way'.[22] While it may be touching that she describes this position as 'noble',[23] Holocaust education surely needs to be based on accuracy, validity and reliability instead. Polak, talking of the work of the Anne Frank House, stated that 'the Diary of Anne Frank can be a useful educational tool for young people working in Muslim majority countries to help them reflect on human rights and issues of tolerance and intolerance'.[24] Not only is this conclusion based on anecdotal evidence derived from presenting their Anne Frank exhibition to countries such as Indonesia, Turkey and Bosnia-Herzegovina, but it is assuming that the Holocaust is able to moralise. Polak, like Peterson, is explicit about this:

> The Anne Frank House, through the exhibition and other educational tools, aims to offer young people the opportunity to learn about Anne Frank and the times she lived in, as a way to think about the importance of working toward a tolerant society in which diversity and the rights of minorities are assured.[25]

Clearly there is no attempt to hide the fact that the work of such NGOs, and the scholarship which derives from them, is resting upon these

DOI: 10.1057/9781137388575.0007

assumptions. In many senses, the blame for building upon unproven foundations ought not to rest upon the organisations who are trying to develop innovative and effective Holocaust education. Instead, the field of Holocaust education as a whole must accept responsibility for not going far enough to try and answer the question of whether or not the Holocaust can moralise learners. While many studies have taken place, they have almost always looked at the immediate, short-term impact of Holocaust education. There have been very few longitudinal studies seeking to analyse how those who have studied the Holocaust are affected in their attitudes and moral decision-making in relation to a control. While no individual study is likely to prove conclusive, carefully designed and large-scale projects are needed. It is admittedly very difficult to know whether Holocaust education was or was not a cause in the evolution of a respondent's attitude or whether other variables were more influential. Yet with a large number of students, which may create trends that reduce the impact of anomalies, carried out over at least a decade and taking into consideration significant variables, useful data might emerge which could strengthen the argument that Holocaust education either does or does not have the capability to moralise and transform learners in a meaningful and lasting way. After all, if Holocaust education only has a transitory, temporary and fleeting impact, then one might legitimately question the money and energy which is being directed into projects which seek to moralise and transform learners. Instead, greater emphasis may need to be focused on issues of remembrance and historical understanding, which are by no means incompatible with those pursuing a moral agenda.

One of the few longitudinal studies which did seek to explore the impact of Holocaust education was conducted by Maitles and Cowan in Scotland, who drew an important distinction between 'immediate' and 'lasting' effects.[26] In this study, they not only tracked the values and attitudes of those who had studied the Holocaust in their early education, but also used a control of similar students who had not studied the subject at primary school. They found that ten months after studying the Holocaust, 'the core sample had stronger positive values and were in the main more tolerant... they were more disposed to active citizenship by their understanding of individual responsibility towards racism'.[27] Interestingly, however, when Maitles and Cowan returned three years later, those who had studied the Holocaust in their early education did not always demonstrate more tolerant or respectful attitudes towards

DOI: 10.1057/9781137388575.0007

various minority groups than the control. In fact gender seemed to be a much more important variation than previous Holocaust education, leading Maitles and Cowan to observe that 'the evidence suggests that... [teaching the Holocaust in primary education] has greater short term benefits than longer term ones'.[28]

Measuring the impact of Holocaust education on the morals and attitudes of learners can especially be difficult for classroom teachers. In a study of teachers in England, the HEDP report found:

> When asked directly what they wanted their students to achieve through a study of the Holocaust, those teachers who prioritised aims such as 'transforming society' or 'tackling racism and prejudice' were likely to answer in terms which would be very difficult to confidently measure or observe.[29]

This suggests that although a number of teachers intend to promote anti-racism through their teaching of the Holocaust, they are by no means confident that they are doing so. This only increases the need for researchers to try and find ways whereby the moral impact of Holocaust education can be measured and observed. It was Cowan and Maitles again who specifically sought to measure the consequences of Holocaust education, by exploring students' responses to visiting Auschwitz. They assessed the practical ways in which students disseminated their experiences within the community with follow-up research forthcoming.[30] These more methodologically rigorous approaches are helpful and are beginning to take the field in a direction that it has long ignored and which may eventually challenge building upon inconclusive assumptions.

While there appears only minimal indication at present that the aims of Holocaust education are increasingly shifting from a moral agenda to a greater focus on historical knowledge and understanding, there do appear a rising number of caveats from those who emphasise the transformative qualities of studying the subject. In 2009, for example, the AFH invited 30 experts in Holocaust education from 12 different countries for a seminar to discuss various opportunities and challenges in the field. Although they accepted the assumption that the Holocaust can improve its learners, they acknowledged that this is also dependent on the nature and delivery of that education.

> Although there are many moral lessons to be learned from the history of the Holocaust, it is counterproductive to lecture about these lessons to young people. They become resistant and dis-interested when they feel they are being preached to.[31]

DOI: 10.1057/9781137388575.0007

As the consequence of a study where Short acknowledged the 'failure' of an initiative aimed at teaching students lessons from genocide, he concluded that:

> The study suggests that for many students in their early to mid-teens, the lessons of the Holocaust will not emerge automatically as they assimilate new knowledge ... It is hard to escape the conclusion that students need help not just in learning *about* the Holocaust but also in learning from it.[32]

Short, one of the greatest advocates of learning from the Holocaust, sees the solution to the 'failure' as making the lessons more explicit. Yet this contrasts with the observations of Hondius who notes:

> Some Holocaust education projects, for instance, have a pronounced moral tone, which can provoke irritation and resistance among students, who tend to dislike being preached to. The end result can be the opposite of what one attempts to accomplish.[33]

It seems apparent that greater scrutiny of existing Holocaust programmes is needed. Riley and Totten correctly argue that teachers unfamiliar with the Holocaust will turn to state-mandated or state-recommended curriculum products as a source of authority and thus their content and aims ought to be critically analysed. Consequently, in their article, 'Understanding Matters: Holocaust Curricula and the Social Studies Classroom', they offer a strong critique of curriculum products in America that lack historical accuracy and depth.[34]

It could be argued that those who advocate students learning from the Holocaust in order that they become improved moral citizens are experiencing a lack of symmetry between their ideological aspirations and the empirical evidence which is emerging.

Objectivity

In addition to requiring a study's sound methodology, there is also an expectation that scholarship will demonstrate the qualities of objectivity, impartiality, detachment and independence. Too often, it would seem research within Holocaust education has not attained these standards.

In the contemporary era of *realpolitik*, where research and publications are so closely connected to public funding, job security and employability, the need for scholarly objectivity is greater than ever. NGOs, charities, museums and other organisations involved in Holocaust education are

DOI: 10.1057/9781137388575.0007

often dependent upon the continued financial support of governments and other major sources of income and this means proving their value. A cynical analysis might suggest that publishing positive accounts of their work, especially in peer-reviewed journals, is an effective marketing tool, which provides it with legitimacy and authority, as well as being a very inexpensive means of reaching the target audience of those involved in the field. Such a position does appear overly cynical yet, for those looking on who are unfamiliar with the field, it is not an unreasonable supposition. Objectivity and impartiality thus cannot be disconnected from validity and reliability. Demonstrating these principles is an integral part of maintaining the quality of scholarship within Holocaust education.

Objectivity is connected to transparency. Researchers need to be explicit in explaining how, for example, the relationship between researcher and participant affected the notion of informed consent and how respondents' knowledge of an organisation's aims affects their evaluative comments. After all, if the director of an organisation which has just provided three days of potentially free training to a teacher interviews them about its impact, are they unlikely to be overly critical? Objectivity is thus connected to methodology, for while it may potentially be suitable for someone working within a Holocaust organisation to assess their own programme's effectiveness, they must do everything possible to limit their influence on the data and acknowledge their biases and limitations.

Such acknowledgements have not been forthcoming in much of the existing research whereby those who are employed by a particular organisation are publishing about the education that they and their colleagues are delivering. Gryglewski, for example, writes about the successes of the educational approaches which are used at the Memorial and Educational Site House of the Wannsee Conference, for which she works. Polak remarks on the way that the Anne Frank House's exhibition and educational resources have encouraged young people to think about tolerance and yet she is a member of their staff. Chyrikins and Vieyra highlight the successes of the work of the AFH in Latin America, where both of them work and according to Chyrikins's biography at the end of her paper, 'since 2003 she has been responsible for the educational programmes of the Anne Frank House in Latin America'.[35] It seems possible that the likes of Gryglewski, Polak or Chyrikins and Vieyra are going to be reluctant in suggesting that their employer's respective educational programmes are not successful, especially seeing that they themselves

DOI: 10.1057/9781137388575.0007

might bear a measure of responsibility for their shortcomings. The potential biases which might be inherent within their thinking are not acknowledged and neither is the fact that vested interest could possibly cloud their perspectives and severely limit their objectivity.

Yet the absence of independence and detachment are evident throughout so much of the scholarship within the field. Shoham et al.'s excellent study of the changing attitudes towards the Holocaust of Arab teachers in Israel provides a very positive analysis and evaluation of the impact of the training course from which the data is derived. Yet the third of the three authors works for the Centre for Humanistic Education, The Ghetto Fighters' Museum in Israel, which was the organisation responsible for organising and running the training course.

Within the United States of America especially, a significant focus of Holocaust education has centred on the work of Facing History and Ourselves (FHAO). Yet scholarly assessments of the effectiveness of their programmes and policies have often been implemented by those who have strong connections to the organisation or who are already strong proponents of it. Riley, Washington and Humphries, in their assessment of FHAO, are critical of the close relationship that those who have conducted research in the programme's effectiveness have had with it. Writing on the research of Melinda Fine, for example, they noted that she 'admits that she developed loyalties to the organization and its staff, which causes her to struggle with the issue of critical perspective as well as giving voice and serious consideration to the viewpoints of *FHAO's* opponents and critics'.[36]

In her article on some of the methods employed by FHAO, Murphy writes, 'teaching the Holocaust in the participatory way that we do ... is a proven, effective way for students to learn this particular history'.[37] Not only is Murphy the Director of International Programs for FHAO, but her only bibliographic reference which could contain this 'proof' to which she alludes is a document which has been published by her own organisation.[38] While this does not mean that the proof is not trustworthy, it does reduce the likelihood of objectivity.

Barr also provides a positive appraisal of the work of FHAO in his article 'Early Adolescents' Reflections on Social Justice: Facing History and Ourselves in Practice And Assessment'. As Director of Evaluation, Barr is in many senses well suited to make such judgements. After all, he is described by his organisation as the one who 'asks "Why?" and "How?" Facing History and Ourselves makes a difference to teachers,

DOI: 10.1057/9781137388575.0007

students, communities and schools past and present – and measures that impact in statistical, quantifiable ways'.[39] Yet there is undoubtedly a lack of objectivity which needs to be acknowledged and an appreciation by those who make such assessments, that their predisposed support for the organisation and its work is probably incompatible with impartial judgements. It seems evident that within the scholarship of Holocaust education, the issue of objectivity needs to be reexamined and greater weight attached to it, especially by those who are publishing about the work of their own organisations.

Dissemination of research

One way of assessing the value of a piece of research is the impact that it has made on the field. In order for the scholarship in Holocaust education to influence teaching and learning it must be disseminated. According to Hargreaves, too often within the field of education, generally, research 'does not make a serious contribution to fundamental theory or knowledge... [and] clutters up academic journals that virtually nobody reads'.[40] Clearly it would seem that if research is to have an impact then it must be read, understood and applied by practitioners who are involved in delivering Holocaust education. Maws suggests that the relationship between Holocaust studies (by which he means scholarship) and Holocaust education (by which he means institutions and practitioners) is by no means what it ought to be.

> 'Holocaust studies' and 'Holocaust education' sound like two concepts which are likely to be very closely related to one another. But, regrettably, the reality is that practitioners in both of these fields too often operate in relative ignorance of each other.[41]

This judgement seems true only to a limited extent. In fact it would appear that Holocaust practitioners are more informed by the research in the field than in most other areas of education. This is principally due to the scale, scope and quality of teacher training in Holocaust education. While access to and funding for such training is certainly limited in some parts of the world, in much of Western Europe and North America there are myriad opportunities for teachers to familiarise themselves with the latest developments in Holocaust scholarship. The same can also be said of Morocco and South Africa, not to mention the opportunities provided

DOI: 10.1057/9781137388575.0007

by various organisations; FHAO, for example, have had educators from over 90 countries attend their courses and worked with practitioners in places like Columbia and Bosnia-Herzegovina.[42] Organisations like the Centre for Holocaust Education in London, the USHMM in Washington DC and Yad Vashem in Jerusalem are not only involved with the training of thousands of teachers each year (both nationally and internationally) but are typically at the forefront of some of the highest quality research which exists within the discipline. Houwink ten Cate acknowledges this when he writes, 'the gap between research output and Holocaust education has been narrowed.'[43]

Maws presents a fascinating angle on the subject, however, when he writes, 'it's not enough for teachers to listen to academics. Academics must, in turn, listen to teachers.'[44] The major studies of teachers' perceptions, experiences and practices of teaching the Holocaust by Lange and the HEDP respectively suggest that to some extent this is taking place but clearly Holocaust educational scholarship needs to ensure that it does not conform to the criticism of Hargreaves when he said that there was a 'yawning gap between theory and practice.'[45] Increasingly, Holocaust scholarship is working alongside practitioners in a symbiotic relationship, and in many parts of the world the field is an excellent example of how the dissemination of research can and ought to take place.

Breadth of research

The quality of scholarship within Holocaust education must also be assessed by its content, by the areas which research has tended to focus upon and the questions it has generally chosen to marginalise or ignore. It seems likely that few within the field would be too critical of the topics explored, even if there could be legitimate criticism of how some studies were conducted. More probable is the frustration with the absence of research in certain areas and the lack of attempts to answer questions which seem most important. Schweber highlights certain voids in the scholarship and emphasises, among other things, the need for further research into museum education and 'how specific audiences learn from the presentations and what they learn in particular'.[46] She also points to the absence of systematic studies in post-secondary Holocaust education and 'calls attention to the need for research devoted specifically to analysis of the expectations, practices, and outcomes of Holocaust education in colleges and universities'.[47]

DOI: 10.1057/9781137388575.0007

Perhaps the most significant omission within the scholarship has been meaningful and thorough investigation into the impact and importance of cultural influences. The ubiquity and universalisation of the Holocaust within some contemporary societies must surely have a significant effect on how teachers interpret, understand and consequently teach the subject in those countries. Practitioners are not immune to shifts in popular thinking which are brought about by the influence of the media, literature and film to name but a few examples. It is not acceptable to assume that because *Schindler's List* seemed to have a big influence 20 years ago, that this remains the case today. The rapid evolution of popular culture has not been sufficiently tracked by Holocaust educational scholarship which has lagged far behind in seeking to assess the significance of films like *The Pianist, Defiance* and *The Boy in the Striped Pyjamas* on teaching and teachers' thinking.

Although there is now beginning to be something of a focus on the importance of students' preconceptions, this has, to date, typically focused on what they already know and not so much on how they acquired their initial ideas. Although Gray's research on the impact of *The Boy in the Striped Pyjamas* is a step in the right direction,[48] it represents but a fraction of what needs to be explored. How much knowledge do pupils acquire from their parents and relations and from their early years education and how significant is its impact in shaping their prior conceptions? Moreover, how easy is it for teachers to change their misconceptions and do they revert back to their original thinking after they have finished their Holocaust education? These practical questions are absolutely central to effective Holocaust education and yet there have been minimal efforts made to try and answer them. While the debates about aims and purposes have been interesting and important, it seems that the arguments have been sufficiently expressed and exhausted without a large degree of consensus. Consequently, it seems pertinent to shift the emphasis of scholarly research into a more practical and empirical direction which recognises the often-forgotten fact that Holocaust education does not exist within a vacuum. It must evolve alongside shifts in popular culture and appreciate that the classroom is only one theatre of learning among many, and when it comes to the Holocaust, it is certainly not the first source of information and perhaps in the cases of some learners, not even the most important. Holocaust education needs to lose its introversion if it is to cope with the dynamic shifts within society and popular culture, both of which frequently engage with the Holocaust as a concept and phenomenon.

DOI: 10.1057/9781137388575.0007

In addition to this, much of the scholarship on the field has lacked a holistic approach. In this regard, the scholarship seems to mirror a lot of school education itself, which often fails to adopt a joined-up approach. It seems that within many institutions the history department is unaware of when and how the Holocaust appears within, say, the English curriculum or the religious studies programme. It seems that greater research is needed on how different subjects can best complement each other and how Holocaust education fits into broader debates within non-traditional disciplines such as sociology and psychology. It seems likely that studies of Judaism in religious studies, for example, might be able to go a long way in tackling ignorance, prejudice and misconceptions towards Jews and Jewish identity and thus have a positive impact of Holocaust education. Moreover, if pupils possess a meaningful understanding of the concept of citizenship within their civics education, they may be in a better position to appreciate the significance of Nazi policies such as the Nuremberg Laws.

Despite the critical approach within this chapter, it is important to remember that there are also examples within the field which exemplify high quality scholarship. Fallace's work on the emergence of Holocaust education in American schools, for instance, demonstrates a holistic approach, which explains the history of American Holocaust education in the broadest possible terms, with reference to popular culture, contemporary scholarship and national sensitivities.[49]

Debates within Holocaust education have far from been exhausted. In fact in some areas, they have not really even begun. Add to that the variations which exist across different countries and cultures, then it seems likely that scholars within the field have a range of unchartered territory to explore in the years ahead.

Conclusion

Scholarship within Holocaust education cannot be viewed as a monolithic entity and there is great variation in the quality of work which has to date been produced. At its best it has been pioneering, innovative and meticulous, while at its worst it has been sterile, repetitive and shoddy. The criticisms contained within this chapter have sought to highlight some all-too-common trends within the field which need addressing and to suggest that the highest possible standards of research ought to

DOI: 10.1057/9781137388575.0007

exist. Future success within Holocaust education is dependent upon the discipline evolving to face the new challenges which are appearing on the horizon. This will only be achieved if the scholarship is robust and rigorous in its methodologies and processes, thorough and strict in its expectations and scrutiny as well as reflective and adaptable in its dissemination and direction.

Notes

1   Chyrikins, M. and Vieyra, M. (2010) 'Making the Past Relevant to Future Generations. The Work of the Anne Frank House in Latin America', *Intercultural Education*, 21: S1, S7–S15, p. S12.
2   Chyrikins and Vieyra, 'Making the Past Relevant', p. S12.
3   Chyrikins and Vieyra, 'Making the Past Relevant', p. S7.
4   Nates, T. (2010) ' "But, Apartheid Was Also Genocide ... What about Our Suffering?" Teaching the Holocaust in South Africa – Opportunities and Challenges', *Intercultural Education*, 21: S1, S17–S26, p. S24.
5   Schweber, S. (2008) ' "What Happened to Their Pets?": Third Graders Encounter the Holocaust', *Teachers College Record*, 110: 10, 2073–2115.
6   Edwards, C. and O'Dowd, S. (2010) 'The Edge of Knowing: Investigating Students' Prior Understandings of the Holocaust', *Teaching History*, 141, 20–26.
7   Rutland, S. (2010) 'Creating Effective Holocaust Education Programmes for Government Schools with Large Muslim Populations in Sydney', *Prospects*, 40: 1, 75–91 and Short, G. (2013) 'Reluctant Learners? Muslim Youth Confront the Holocaust', *Intercultural Education*, 24: 1–2, 121–132.
8   Von Borries, B. (2003) 'Attitudes of Teachers and Pupils towards the Shoa in Germany', *Intercultural Education*, 14: 2, 201–214, p. 207.
9   De Vaus, D. (2007) *Surveys in Social Research*, (London: Routledge), p. 99.
10 Bischoping, K. (1998) 'Method and Meaning in Holocaust-Knowledge Surveys', *Holocaust and Genocide Studies*, 12: 3, 454–474, p. 455.
11 Bischoping, 'Method and Meaning', p. 455.
12 London Jewish Cultural Centre (2009) 'Full Scale of Holocaust Unknown to British Children', Press Release.
13 Golub, J. and Cohen, R. (1993) *What do Americans know about the Holocaust?* (New York: American Jewish Committee).
14 The question asked, 'Does it seem possible or does it seem impossible to you that the Nazi extermination of the Jews never happened?'
15 The revised question asked, 'Does it seem possible to you that the Nazi extermination of the Jews never happened, or do you feel certain that it happened?'

DOI: 10.1057/9781137388575.0007

16   Smith, T. (1995) *Holocaust Denial: What the Survey Data Reveal*, (New York: American Jewish Committee).

17   Kinloch, N. (2001) 'Parallel Catastrophes? Uniqueness, Redemption and the Shoah', *Teaching History*, 104, 8–14.

18   Novick, P. (1999) *The Holocaust in American Life*, (New York: Houghton Mifflin Co.).

19   Eckmann, M. (2010) 'Exploring the Relevance of Holocaust Education for Human Rights Education', *Prospects*, 40: 17–16.

20   Short, G. (2003) 'Lessons of the Holocaust: A Response to the Critics', *Educational Review*, 55: 3, 277–287.

21   Cowan, P. and Maitles, H. (2007) 'Does Addressing Prejudice and Discrimination through Holocaust Education Produce Better Citizens?', *Educational Review*, 59: 2, 115–130.

22   Peterson, T. (2010) 'Moving beyond the Toolbox: Teaching Human Rights through Teaching the Holocaust in Post-Apartheid South Africa', *Intercultural Education*, 21, S1, S27–S31, p. S28.

23   Peterson, 'Moving beyond the Toolbox', p. S28.

24   Polak, K. (2010) 'Tolerance Education in Morocco. "Anne Frank: A History for Today": Learning about Our Past – Contributing to Our Future', *Intercultural Education*, 21: S1, S51–S59, p. S57.

25   Polak, 'Tolerance Education in Morocco', p. S57.

26   Maitles, H. and Cowan, P. (2008) 'More Open to Diversity?: The Longer Term Citizenship Impact of Learning about the Holocaust', in Reflecting on Identities: Research, Practice and Innovation. Children's Identity and Citizenship in Europe, London, 521–530. ISBN 978-0-9560454-7-8, 525–526, p. 525.

27   Maitles and Cowan, 'More Open to Diversity?', pp. 525–526.

28   Maitles and Cowan, 'More Open to Diversity?', p. 528.

29   Pettigrew, A., Foster, S., Howson, J., Salmons, P., Lenga, R- A. and Andrews, K. (2009) *Teaching about the Holocaust in English Secondary Schools: An Empirical Study of National Trends, Perspectives and Practice*, (Holocaust Education Development Programme, Institute of Education, University of London), p. 86.

30   Cowan, P. and Maitles, H. (2011) ' "We Saw Inhumanity Close Up". What Is Gained by School Students from Scotland Visiting Auschwitz?', *Journal of Curriculum Studies*, 43: 2, 163–184.

31   Van Driel, B. and Van Dijk, L. (2010) 'Diverse Classrooms – Opportunities and Challenges', *Intercultural Education*, 21: S1, S1–S5, p. S2.

32   Short, G. (2005) 'Learning from Genocide? A Study in the Failure of Holocaust Education', *Intercultural Education*, 16: 4, 367–380, p. 378.

33   Hondius, D. (2010) 'Finding Common Good in Education about the Holocaust and Slavery', *Intercultural Education*, 21: S1, S61–S69, p. S64.

DOI: 10.1057/9781137388575.0007

34 Riley, K. and Totten, S. (2002) 'Understanding Matters: Holocaust Curricula and the Social Studies Classroom', *Theory and Research in Social Education*, 30: 4, 541–562.

35 Chyrikins and Vieyra, 'Making the Past Relevant', p. S14.

36 Riley, K., Washington, E. and Humphries, E. (2011) 'Facing History and Ourselves: Noble Purpose, Unending Controversy', in Totten, S. and Pedersen, J. (Eds) *Teaching and Studying Social Issues: Major Programs and Approaches*, (Charlotte, North Carolina: Information Age Publishing), pp. 119–139, p. 124.

37 Murphy, K. (2010) 'Example of Best Practice 1. Teaching a Holocaust Case Study in a Post-Conflict Environment: Education as Part of Violence, Reconstruction and Repair', *Intercultural Education*, 21: S1, S71–S77, p. S76.

38 Strom, M. and Parsons, W. S. (1984) *Facing History and Ourselves: Holocaust and Human Behaviour*, (New York: Facing History and Ourselves National Foundation).

39 www.facinghistory.org/about/who/profiles/we-change-lives-he-measures-how. Accessed 23 August 2013.

40 Hargreaves, D. (1996) *Teaching as a Research-Based Profession: Possibilities and Prospects*, (London: Teacher Training Agency), p. 7.

41 Andrews, K., Gray, M. and Maws, A. (2013) 'Responses to BJ Epstein's "Inflicting Trauma"', *Holocaust Studies: A Journal of Culture and History*, 19: 1, 121–134, p. 130.

42 Murphy, 'Examples of Best Practice', p. S71.

43 Houwink ten Cate, J. (2010) 'The Future of Holocaust Studies', *Jewish Political Studies Review*, 22: 1–2, 33–41, p. 37.

44 Andrews, Gray and Maws, 'Responses', p. 130.

45 Hargreaves, *Teaching as a Research-Based Profession*, p. 2.

46 Schweber, S. (2010) 'Education' in Hayes, P. and Roth, J. (Eds) *The Oxford Handbook of Holocaust Studies*, (Oxford: Oxford University Press), 695–708, p. 701.

47 Schweber, 'Education', p. 701.

48 Gray, M. (2013) 'The Boy in the Striped Pyjamas: A Blessing or Curse for Holocaust Educators?', Paper presented at *The Future of Holocaust Studies Conference*, Universities of Southampton and Winchester, 29–31 July 2013.

49 Fallace, T. (2008) *The Emergence of Holocaust Education in American Schools*, (New York: Palgrave Macmillan).

DOI: 10.1057/9781137388575.0007

4
Holocaust Universalisation

Abstract: *Drawing upon multidisciplinary scholarship on Holocaust universalisation, this chapter analyses and evaluates the pedagogic impact of this important sociological development. Consequently it argues that the sanctity of the Holocaust no longer exists for many within education. In addition to this, the ubiquity of the Holocaust as a cultural reference has aided its trivialisation and de-Judaisation. Holocaust universalisation has also led to shifts in the way that the Holocaust is taught, with an increased used of multidisciplinary and thematic teaching which draws upon the Holocaust in a range of subjects and uses it as just one example of genocide or human rights abuses.*

Keywords: de-Judaisation; genocide; sanctity; thematic learning; universalisation

Gray, Michael. *Contemporary Debates in Holocaust Education.* Basingstoke: Palgrave Macmillan, 2014. DOI: 10.1057/9781137388575.0008.

DOI: 10.1057/9781137388575.0008

The question of whether or not the Holocaust is unique directly relates to whether it provides moral lessons that must be taught to contemporary society. In that regard, especially, this controversy is very relevant for Holocaust education. When discussing the question of the Holocaust's uniqueness, the parameters of the discourse have characteristically been limited to historical or semantic arguments and this too has been reflected in the nature of pedagogic scholarship on the issue.

At the beginning of the twenty-first century, the confines of the discussion shifted, principally, due to the valuable contribution of scholarship which adopted a sociological perspective. One of the principle catalysts for this new approach came from J.C. Alexander's paper, 'On the Social Construction of Moral Universals: The "Holocaust" from War Crime to Trauma Drama', which Hartman described as an 'already classic essay'.[1] Alexander, among other things, explains the paradox that exists between the particularism and universalism of the Holocaust within a socio-cultural framework. He highlights how within popular Western consciousness the idea that 'the Holocaust was a unique event in human history crystallized' and that it eventually came to be perceived to be the ultimate symbol of evil. Yet as a consequence of that, 'its moral implications became paradoxically generalized'[2] characterised by the fact that 'major urban centers in the United States, and many outside it as well, constructed vastly expensive, and vastly expansive, museums to make permanent its moral lessons.'[3]

Yet sociological and culturally related notions of universalism go beyond the morality upon which Alexander was focusing. Levy and Sznaider, for example, argue that the *memory* of the Holocaust has become universalised and now goes beyond the traditional boundaries of the nation state in what they describe as 'cosmopolitan memory'. They suggest that 'shared memories of the Holocaust...provide the foundations for a new cosmopolitan memory, a memory transcending ethnic and national boundaries.'[4] Although Hirsch and Spitzer see their position as possibly a little too optimistic,[5] Levy and Sznaider perceptively acknowledge that cosmopolitan memory does not signify that the Holocaust has an identical meaning for everyone. Certainly the relationship between Holocaust education and national consciousness, as discussed in Chapter 2, would support that idea.

Connected to concepts of morality and memory is the universalism of Holocaust consciousness. Pearce has demonstrated how in Britain, for example, 'the Holocaust is a pervasive presence in British culture and society'.[6] Yablonka, focusing on particular court cases, also begins to highlight the development of Holocaust consciousness in Israel and its increasing importance within public thinking.[7] Moses shows the strength of Holocaust consciousness in Australia, especially among the political right,[8] although Caldwell writes of New Zealand's Holocaust consciousness that it was late in starting and 'not as developed or comprehensive as in other countries'.[9] It thus seems fair to say that in terms of morality, memory and public consciousness in many parts of the world the Holocaust has become universalised.

This is characterised by the ubiquity of the Holocaust in many modern cultures. Not only can one visit a Children's Holocaust Memorial in Whitwell, Tennessee, a community of around 1600 people, none of whom are Jewish and which is several thousand miles away from the location of the Nazi murders,[10] but one can also find video conferencing from Mémorial de la Shoah being broadcast to 'students, teachers and lawyers in Madagascar, Togo, Burundi, Cameroon, the Democratic Republic of Congo and Senegal'.[11]

The ever-increasing universalisation of the Holocaust poses many questions for Holocaust education and this chapter seeks to explore some of the potential implications of this socio-cultural evolution.

The sanctity of the Holocaust

The seeming ubiquity of the Holocaust within the social consciousness and cultural discourse of many countries has the potential of turning the sacred into the common. For many students, the subject is no longer shrouded in reverential awe but a theme which has appeared on their curriculum on many previous occasions and been witnessed through film, literature and the media. Schweber observes that, in her experiences, significant changes have taken place in the approach of her pupils.

> I recall that, years ago, my students approached the subject with a kind of inbred reverence, a seriousness and cautiousness that bordered on nervousness. They handled the topic gingerly, as if it could shatter... I find that my students now tend to approach the Holocaust without that pause, without a default position of veneration. The Holocaust is, for them, interesting but not awesome.[12]

This shift away from the sanctification of the Holocaust may lead practitioners to push the boundaries further in an attempt to generate that awe

DOI: 10.1057/9781137388575.0008

and to produce an emotional response. This poses problems and Salmons is correct in noting that 'we need strategies for moving students without traumatising them, for ensuring they understand the enormity of the events without titillating or horrifying them with graphic images.'[13]

Whereas Schweber used to worry that learning about the Holocaust was obstructed by the reverence of pupils, she writes that, 'I now worry that trivialization of the Holocaust impedes its understanding.'[14] What might be considered characteristic of this is the increasing number of 'collecting projects', where typically children collect six million of a specific object to represent each of the Jews who were murdered by the Nazi regime and their collaborators. This has been especially common in America, for example the collecting of paper butterflies in the Holocaust Museum in Houston or the collecting of six million buttons by the Jewish Federation of Peoria, Illinois.[15] Magilov writes of such projects that 'to collect millions of inanimate objects... will surely always strike some as a tacky and trivializing approach to memorializing the Holocaust.' Yet he argues that it represents a new approach to a very difficult process of memory and offers a balanced and thoughtful reflection of the subject.[16]

Holocaust trivialisation is often generated by comparing the Holocaust to contemporary events, often for a specific purpose. Salmons acknowledges that 'the power of the Holocaust as a motif, a metaphor or a rhetorical device, is used to advocate a bewildering array of special interests, social and political agendas.'[17] Opponents of greater gun control in America for example have suggested that the Nazis' 1938 firearm registration in Germany helped facilitate the Holocaust[18] while according to the BBC, John Paul II in 2005 likened abortion to the Holocaust.[19] Especially controversial was the 'Holocaust on your Plate' campaign led by People for the Ethical Treatment of Animals.[20] Their displays contrasted images of caged animals with camp inmates and was banned in Germany by its High Court, stating that it made 'the fate of the victims of the Holocaust appear banal and trivial.'[21] It is this abuse of the term 'Holocaust', which is given by Cohen as one reason among many, as to why the term Shoah is more preferable. He states:

> Recently the word *holocaust* has been invoked in protests against any number of social and political issues, some of which have no relation to genocide (i.e. environmental problems, crime, abortion, animal slaughter, assimilation and intermarriage, deaths from tobacco use etc.). The word *Shoah* may be understood as referring to the Nazi's institutionalized mass murder, particularly of the Jews of Europe.[22]

DOI: 10.1057/9781137388575.0008

Holocaust trivialisation is perhaps one of the most important challenges which contemporary educators have to face. This was acknowledged in an article in *The Economist* in 2013, which stated that 'perhaps
the biggest threat to remembrance of the 6m Jews killed by the Nazis
is trivialisation'.[23] It is difficult to know the extent to which young
people are influenced by Holocaust references in the media and in
popular culture, but the existing work on preconceptions would suggest that they assimilate a lot of ideas into their prior conceptions.
There is no evidence that this use of the Holocaust as a metaphor is
likely to decrease and thus it seems probable that for many students
the Holocaust will remain trivialised, universalised and generalised
which removes its sense of sanctity and differentness.

Perhaps the extreme antonymic example of Holocaust sanctification is Holocaust humour. Rabbi Block, writing about America, stated
that 'Holocaust jokes' are 'horrifying, depraved attempts at humour'
which 'our children are hearing' and which are a 'serious problem that
plagues our society and culture'.[24] Holocaust jokes are connected but
by no means the same thing as Holocaust humour. Solomon wrote of
Holocaust art, for example, that 'the use of humour ... is uniquely suited
to the representation of an event so inherently absurd and terrifying'.[25]
Yet can there be any compatibility between appropriate humour and
the Holocaust in the classroom? In a fascinating study conducted on
55 Holocaust survivors, Ostrower asked respondents 'can you describe
or tell about, humour in the Holocaust?' The findings not only highlighted the frequency and importance of humour but suggested that on
60 per cent of occasions, humour was used as a defence mechanism.[26]
It is thus possible that when pupils adopt a 'light-hearted' approach to
studying the Holocaust that they too are doing so because they do not
feel comfortable with the emotional situation in which they find themselves. In his study of responses to Holocaust education in England,
Richardson observed how one boy was 'using humour as a means
of managing potentially difficult knowledge'.[27] Incidentally, this was
because he was concerned about his German friend. This seems very
different from Holocaust or anti-Semitic 'jokes'. Whereas the former
is possibly a defensive barrier due to the sacredness (and potential
awkwardness) of the subject, the latter is due to ignorance, prejudice or
the desanctification of the Holocaust which has potentially emerged as
a consequence of its universalisation.

DOI: 10.1057/9781137388575.0008

Cultural influences

The universalisation of the Holocaust is perhaps most apparent within popular Western culture, much of which is exported throughout the world. Bauer writes that, 'hardly a month passes without a new TV production, a new film, a number of new books of prose or poetry dealing with the subject, and the flood is increasing rather than abating.'[28] This is evident by the fact that out of the 16,000 books on the subject which are catalogued in the Library of Congress, over two-thirds of them were published in the last 20 years.[29] Such an increase of Holocaust representation creates problems. Anna Richardson observed a 'tension between ethics and aesthetics inherent in an act of artistic production that reproduces the cultural values of the society that generated the Holocaust.'[30] Salmons too acknowledges this when he writes, 'what is at stake is not whether we choose to remember, but what form that memory takes.'[31]

Haggith and Newman write that, 'paradoxically, it has been those films that have been most successful in creating a mass awareness of the Holocaust (*Holocaust* (1978), *Schindler's List* (1993)) that have caused so much pain and anger among the survivor community.'[32] Such productions certainly call into question how we remember the Holocaust although there can be little doubt that they have been hugely influential on Holocaust education. Doneson writes:

> Educators should have been the ones to ensure that the Holocaust was taught to new generations. But that simply did not happen. Various studies indicate that for at least some thirty years after the war, in all educational areas – religion, social studies, history – in secondary schools as well as universities, most texts either minimally treated the Holocaust or ignored it all together. In the 1990s and into the new millennium, for better or for worse, Holocaust education has become *de rigeur* in conjunction with the study of history at a good many secondary schools. One suspects that this... is the result, in part, of the influence of media representations of the event.[33]

It seems only correct for Doneson to place an important emphasis on popular culture and the media representations of the Holocaust. Nevertheless, the influence of the *Facing History and Ourselves* programme ought not to be marginalised, in terms of its influence and significance within both American and global Holocaust education. In addition to receiving federal funding and being one of the first major programmes in America, its curricula have also shifted over the decades

DOI: 10.1057/9781137388575.0008

in what has either been a cause or characteristic of increased Holocaust universalisation. According to Riley, Washington and Humphries, the revised curriculum of 1982 'moved much farther away from the actual history of the Holocaust than the 1976 version'[34] and 'in the curricular sense, *FHAO* or *Facing History* belongs in a sociological classroom rather than the history classroom'.[35] It is difficult to know how much FHAO has influenced American society and culture and vice versa.

Nevertheless, the recent shifts in Holocaust consciousness, which Doneson expresses regarding America, are equally valid were they to be applied to other countries such as England, where the Holocaust became a statutory part of the National Curriculum in 1991. Perhaps therefore, the most important impact of Holocaust universalisation is that the Holocaust is now popularly perceived to be a key component of a liberal education.

Yet in addition to simply establishing the educational significance of the Holocaust, the universalisation of the subject through popular culture has helped to shape students' thinking on the topic. As demonstrated in Chapter 1, children do arrive in the classroom with a wide range of conceptions and ideas, many of which have been acquired through the media. Speaking of her school visits after what has sometimes been described as the *Schindler's List* effect, survivor Rudy Kennedy said, 'you could then go to schools to talk to the children about it, and we found that we didn't have to start at the beginning: do you know the Holocaust? Do you know what it means?'[36] Kennedy goes onto highlight the increase in children's preconceptions over the years by observing, 'it was the Schindler film that broke the silence... the children have seen much more, know much more.'[37]

Gray's recent study on contemporary children's preconceptions found that *The Boy in the Striped Pyjamas* was both more influential and more commonly seen than the likes of *Schindler's List*.[38] He noted '*The Boy in the Striped Pyjamas* is now probably one of the most important mediums whereby pupils encounter and understand the Holocaust',[39] with 75.8 per cent of his 298 pupil sample having either read the book or watched the film. Conversely, only 9.7 per cent had seen *Schindler's List*. Gray provided examples of how many young people see the story, with one respondent, for example, stating, 'I read *The Boy in the Striped Pyjamas*. I learnt a lot about concentration camps from this.'[40] Moreover, Gray concluded that 'many thirteen and fourteen year olds are not able to differentiate effectively when fiction is situated in a historical setting'[41] and

DOI: 10.1057/9781137388575.0008

thus the story establishes a number of problematic misconceptions. This was characterised by a boys' response to the question of why the Holocaust ended when he said, 'I think it ended when one of the Nazi children died in the poisonous gas in the Jew camp.'[42]

The influence of popular culture and especially cinematic interpretations of the Holocaust seem important throughout much of the world. One of the directors of the Holocaust museum in Mexico (Memory and Tolerance), which opened in 2010, stated that 'there is very little Holocaust education and most Mexicans' knowledge of the Holocaust comes from Hollywood movies.'[43] Moreover, 'Japanese interest in the Holocaust increased after the international release of *Schindler's List*.'[44] Fallace recognised the impact of *Schindler's List* and popular culture on American Holocaust consciousness as well.[45]

Yet cultural devices such as books and films are not only important in establishing preconceptions. Within the process of formal classroom learning, the use and influence of artistic representation is also very common and many teachers read books and show films to their students. Santerini, speaking of Holocaust education in Italy, writes that 'the majority of students learn about the history of the Holocaust through the texts, films, lectures, presentations, discussions, etc. they are exposed to at school.'[46] He also observes that:

> In Italy, as was the case in many other countries, Steven Spielberg's *Schindler's List* became a defining moment in the new generation's awareness of the Holocaust... At the end of the 1990s, the Italian film *Life Is Beautiful* by Roberto Benigni signified perhaps another and controversial turning point [47]

In the findings of the HEDP in England, the most commonly cited resource for teaching about the subject was *Schindler's List*, with 51 of the 127 practitioners who mentioned it stating that it was their most useful resource of all. In fact 76 per cent (n.765) of teachers 'said they were likely to use feature films about the Holocaust' including *The Pianist* and *The Boy in the Striped Pyjamas*.[48] It is noteworthy that the HEDP research was conducted just after the release of *The Boy in the Striped Pyjamas* and thus it is possible that its full impact was not yet evident.

In a localised study in England, McIntyre found that the 2002 film *The Pianist*, which was shown to pupils in lessons, was particularly impactful on their thinking. McIntyre notes, 'it may be that the visual and dramatic power of the film *The Pianist* had a disproportionate impact, compared

DOI: 10.1057/9781137388575.0008

with other teaching approaches, as a means of conveying knowledge about events to some students.'[49] In his article on the use of Holocaust film in the classroom, Morgan goes as far as to say that 'film is how the vast majority of the population, young and old, experience history, whether through enjoying feature film as entertainment or, increasingly, recording their own lives and world through audiovisual means.'[50]

Empirical research on the impact of popular culture on students is surprisingly rare. Typically, analysis of Holocaust representation has focused on either artistic criticism or ethical debates. Almost all of these discussions have revolved around theoretical arguments and ignored attempts to assess the actual impact of such films on perceptions and understanding. It is thus very difficult to assess with any real confidence the significance of the Holocaust's universalisation through popular culture. Yet the available evidence would suggest that it is instrumental in not only forming pupils' initial understandings, but both during and after their official schooling. With limited curriculum time and with many students stopping their study of history in their early teenage years, it is often culture and not the classroom which shapes understanding. Rensmann said of German students' experiences, for example, that 'after 10th grade they don't have to take history classes any anymore. This means that the media and private conversations may be more important and influential resources of "Holocaust education" than German schools.'[51] It certainly seems the case that Holocaust universalisation within popular culture has been instrumental in establishing the centrality of Holocaust education within the curriculum and, in many cases, also the nature of learning that takes place.

A multidisciplinary education

It is surely quite peculiar that the Holocaust and its memory are perceived to be so important in countries like America and England, which appear geographically and historically removed from the killings themselves. This situation highlights the pertinence of Levy and Sznaider's concept of 'cosmopolitan memory'. In such cases, the contemporary relevance of the Holocaust has often needed constructing. Stevick and Michaels write that:

> The lack of a direct link to the Holocaust in many parts of the world means that its relevance must be established, interpreted, and argued; these

DOI: 10.1057/9781137388575.0008

processes of comparison and of meaning-making are key elements in the universalization and globalization of Holocaust education.[52]

Meaning and significance are often provided to the Holocaust by giving it various pedagogic functions. One of the most important of these within Western education has been as a device for the promotion of liberal values, tolerance, respect, anti-racism and human rights. Cole critically suggests that 'given its mythical status, the "Holocaust" risks becoming a popular past used to serve all sorts of present needs. In particular, the needs of contemporary liberalism tends to latch onto a powerful tale in the past and universalize it so as to produce a set of universal lessons.'[53]

This universalising of the so-called lessons, places on the Holocaust an intrinsic functional value; it also attempts to imbibe the subject with a contemporary relevance which transcends generations and to some extent, even subject disciplines. It also helps to justify studying the Holocaust over other genocides or human rights abuses due to its perceived purpose and utility.

A product of this educational universalisation is that the Holocaust is now taught across a range of academic disciplines. While this raises issues about the knowledge of non-history specialists, it seems appropriate that the history department within an institution does not claim to have a monopoly on the subject. Bauer remarked that:

> The historian's art is, after all, limited, and the writer, the poet, the artist, the dramatist, the musician, the psychologist, and, for the religious among us, the theologian have to be asked to add their insights.[54]

Within an educational context the same sentiment is often perceived to be true. Balberg writes:

> When dealing with the major issues related to the impact of the Holocaust in our time one should go beyond just studying history. It enables educators to look into the meaning of the Holocaust for the conscience of humanity and also to discover the proper ways to assist the younger generations to internalize and analyze it lessons. ... The purpose here is not to replace the study of the history of the Holocaust as the main discipline. Non-historical representations of the Holocaust can only enhance the exploration and analysis of the deeper aspects of this major event in the history of mankind.[55]

It is thus not uncommon for students to study a piece of Holocaust fiction in literature classes, or consider the subject in religious studies when contemplating concepts of evil or to work on a play in drama which is

DOI: 10.1057/9781137388575.0008

set within the context of the Holocaust. In the HEDP study, it was noted that history and religious studies were the most common subjects where the Holocaust was taught but some of their respondents talked about teaching the subject in a very wide range of disciplines.

> Small numbers of teachers reported that they taught about the Holocaust within a variety of different and perhaps unexpected subject areas including philosophy, psychology, science, maths, ICT and business studies as well as general studies and combined humanities. The survey also received responses from a small number of individuals whose teaching about the Holocaust was not subject-based – such as special educational needs co-ordinators – or was concentrated in extra-curricular activities, including school assemblies.[56]

It seems unlikely that 30 years ago such a broad sweep of subjects might even on occasions teach about the Holocaust and this seems symptomatic of Holocaust universalisation. Yet the HEDP data revealed some concerning trends. For pupils in England aged between 11–13, they were most likely to encounter the Holocaust in a subject other than history. Yet unsurprisingly, the levels of knowledge about the Holocaust held by non-history specialists was significantly lower than those who were history specialists. Only 7 per cent of those teaching Personal Social Health Education (PSHE) thought that the systematic mass murder of the Jewish people began in 1941 with the invasion of the Soviet Union – a fact which was known by 49 per cent of history teachers.[57] It is thus possible that the universalisation of the Holocaust has led to the subject being encountered and taught in different ways, but often by those with less knowledge and understanding of the history of the Holocaust.

A similar situation emerged from Lange's data in Sweden, where he noted that history teachers in upper secondary schools felt more confident in their knowledge of the Holocaust than history specialists in primary schools or non-history specialists in upper secondary schools. Teachers of physical education felt the least confident in their knowledge.[58] In compiling a weighted index of teacher knowledge, 18.4 per cent of upper secondary school teachers scored in the top tier, compared with 8.0 per cent of history teachers irrespective of age and only 3.9 per cent of all teachers. This data might suggest that Holocaust universalisation and the teaching of the subject within various fields may well broaden students' experiences and perceptions of the Holocaust, but comes at the cost of being taught by those who may be deficient in their historical knowledge of the subject.

DOI: 10.1057/9781137388575.0008

By teaching it within a range of disciplines, the Holocaust is universalised. This is seen in terms of its morality within religious education
and in terms of its 'moralising qualities' within civics-based education.
In practical terms this typically means making comparisons between
the Holocaust and other events or relating specific circumstances and
scenarios to contemporary situations, so that appropriate lessons can be
learned. Short, for example, suggests that 'when they [students] learn
about the exploits of rescuers, they will find it hard not to appreciate
the value of assisting those in need.'[59] While such a concept and application is virtuous, there is surely a danger that such comparisons can be
problematic. The plight of a Jewish family fleeing the Nazis' policy of
mass murder is not the same as a child being teased in the playground.
The consequences of assisting such a victim (for both the victims and
the rescuer) is not comparable either and there is a danger that pupils
will learn to see decision-making processes as simplistic and void of
historical context and empathy. The Holocaust was not a severe form of
bullying, but rather a systematic policy of extermination and attempts to
liken the two risk grave trivialisation and decontextualisation of a very
complex historical phenomenon. This is not to say that a student cannot
be inspired by a Schindler or a Wallenberg, perhaps even inspired enough
to act differently, but this is not the same thing as making a direct and
immediate comparison between 1940s Europe and the school playing
fields. It is important that practitioners are not guilty of what Eckmann
describes as 'putting the lessons of history before the knowledge of the
history itself'.[60]

Perhaps more appropriate are comparisons between the Holocaust
and other genocides and human rights atrocities. Yet these must surely
be historically grounded and demonstrate far greater sophistication and
contextualisation than a crass assessment of which group suffered more
or were killed on a larger scale. The ITF guidelines on comparative genocide wisely caution that such studies ought 'not to equate, diminish, or
trivialise either the Holocaust or the genocides to which the Holocaust
is compared'.[61]

Thematic teaching

The increasing comparisons which are made between the Holocaust
and other genocides or human rights abuses has not only led to the

DOI: 10.1057/9781137388575.0008

Holocaust being taught in more subjects, but it has shifted the way that it is taught within history lessons. In Europe and America, for example, the Holocaust has typically been studied in history as part of broader courses on Germany, Europe, or the Second World War. In other words, there has been a chronological approach. This method has helped students to place the Holocaust in context and understand it more effectively. After all, how can one appreciate the geography or the ending of the Holocaust without awareness of the Second World War? Yet increasingly, a chronological approach is being replaced by a thematic approach, often as a consequence of trying to justify the relevance of the Holocaust on the curriculum. Eckmann writes:

> Teachers also find it difficult to answer questions such as 'Why are you always speaking about Jews?' and 'Why not speak about Rwanda, about slavery or about the Roma?' Or, in post-Soviet countries they might ask, 'Why not speak about the Gulag?' In Western European contexts, we observed that such questions lead teachers to adopt new strategies...more and more educators, especially in the upper grades, tend to teach it within the context of comparing genocides, or within the context of topics like racism, totalitarianism, and colonialism.

Such an approach has at times been associated with the American Holocaust programme, *Facing History and Ourselves*. Rather than adopting a historically grounded and chronological approach, FHAO has often been issues-driven, which has been the cause of criticism among certain scholars such as Riley, Washington and Humphries.[62]

A thematic approach risks the possibility of failing to ground the Holocaust in sufficient historical context. The Holocaust cannot be understood by simply seeing it as 'extreme racism' anymore than the Rwandan genocide can be perceived simply as a consequence of colonialism. What Eckmann is referring to has been described by others, like Hondius, as 'conceptual history', which 'has had a significant impact in Germany and across Europe, where scholars and educators have found its methods inspiring in helping to discuss and explain social change'.[63] Hondius states that she 'recommends a broad, general, inclusive, conceptual approach as a framework for teaching, and a relevant and balanced selection of individual, local and personal histories as illuminating case studies'.[64] There appear to be problems with such a recommendation. Perhaps the most important of these is that one cannot fully understand concepts such as racism or genocide until they are understood within the context of specific historical examples which go beyond broadness

DOI: 10.1057/9781137388575.0008

and generalisation. Moreover, while case studies are of great value in understanding both the Holocaust and the past more generally, one must also recognise that such examples must be representative and not merely selected and then taken out of context to support a 'lesson' which one might want to learn from the Holocaust.

Explaining the Holocaust

The universalisation of the Holocaust as the absolute evil from which 'lessons' are to be drawn often marginalises attempts at historical explanations of the Holocaust, questions such as why it happened, how anti-Semitism became genocide and why people were willing to participate in such murderous policies. Salmons is critical of this approach and states that 'if we simply turn it into a metaphor for the "lessons" we wish young people to learn, then we deprive them of the opportunity to ask the challenging and difficult questions that come from the specificity of the event itself.'[65] Bialystok too expresses disapproval of pedagogy which fails to address the historical explanations when he writes that 'the weak est curricula... resist the mandate to teach. Their approach is grounded in asking the student "How do you feel?" rather than demanding "What do you know?" The key to learning about the Holocaust is knowledge, as it is about any other topic.'[66] Salmons also suggests that the study of the Holocaust as history is often 'afforded a relatively low status even among many history teachers'.[67] A potential consequence of universalisation is thus not only an absence in students to understand but also of educators to teach understanding. Consequently, it seems, Fallace is correct when he asserts, 'students should learn about the historical particularities of all these events in their full historical context.'[68]

Yet it is not just the Holocaust itself but also its relevance which educators have to try and explain; something which can be especially challenging in multicultural classrooms, in countries outside of Europe. Eckmann's comment about teachers finding it difficult to explain why the Holocaust is being studied rather than a different atrocity raises some important issues. It suggests that the special status that the Holocaust is given as the universal symbol of evil and the key component within cosmopolitan memory is not always shared or understood. Nates observes that 'participants in South African educator workshops focusing on teaching the Holocaust and the 1994 genocide in Rwanda frequently

DOI: 10.1057/9781137388575.0008

declare that apartheid was also genocide', as though they are uncomfortable with the special status given to the Holocaust.[69] Teachers and
students within some communities in America have argued that a study
of slavery is much more relevant than the Holocaust. Such reactions are
both a product of universalisation and a challenge to it. Without this
universalisation, students and teachers would perhaps not feel that the
Holocaust was too dominant in education. Yet it is also a challenge, for
it seems to resist the mainstream cultural discourse, which increasingly
sees the Holocaust as a defining phenomenon within history, anthropology, ethics, theology and so many other fields of study.

De-Judaisation

A consequence of comparing the Holocaust to other events and of
Holocaust universalisation more generally is the potential of marginalis-
ing the Jewish specificity of the phenomenon. While in some senses this
relates to semantics and whether the term 'Holocaust' is used to refer
only to Jewish victims of Nazi persecution or all social, political and
ethnic groups. Nevertheless, what might be described as 'de-Judaisation'
of the Holocaust goes beyond definitions and relates to how memory
and meaning is attached to the past. In his thoughtful discussion of the
subject, Gerstenfeld emphasises that the de-Judaisation of the Holocaust
should 'not be confused with the laudable effort to draw conclusions
for all humanity from the genocidal catastrophe caused to the Jewish
people. One major aspect of humanity at large trying to integrate the
Holocaust's lessons into moral standards, is its having become an icon of
absolute evil in many societies.'[70] Instead, Gerstenfeld suggests examples
of de-Judaisation might include attempts 'to rob the Jews of their painful memories or to weaken their perceived hold on the memory of this
genocide.'[71] Similarly, he highlights erroneous historical presentations
of the past, such as suggesting that the Jews were 'accidental victims'
of the Holocaust, which was somehow a natural consequence of Nazi
expansionist policies and 'wartime brutalisation'.[72] Moreover, Holocaust
education ought to include how the collective treatment of the Jews
was uniquely different to other victims of Nazi persecution. Preventing
de-Judaisation thus relies on accurate historical knowledge and sound
understanding. If Holocaust universalisation means that the subject is

increasingly being taught by non-history specialists, as evidence would suggest, then it may lead to the increase of de-Judaisation.

Within many popular cultural representations of the Holocaust, possibly due to attempts to market a product to a wider audience, there has been what might be referred to as de-Judaisation. This has often been typified by telling stories about the Holocaust which revolve around non-Jewish protagonists or marginalise the Jewishness of the characters. In *Schindler's List*, for example, the leading figure is a German. In *Sophie's Choice* the victim is a Polish Catholic while within the representations of Anne Frank, her Jewish culture and religion has normally been overlooked. It is particularly the use of Anne Frank as a symbol of generalised rather than Jewish suffering which has characterised both the universalisation and the consequent de-Judaisation of the Holocaust. Barnouw states that 'Anne Frank is by now more a symbol of the universal suffering of man than "the voice of six million vanished souls"'.[73] Characteristic of this is the life-sized bust of Anne Frank outside the British Library in London with a commemorative tree planted a few feet away. The inscription accompanying this memorial states that it is there 'to commemorate Anne Frank and all the children killed in wars and conflict in this century'. Yet Anne Frank's death was not an accident of war, but rather a systematic murder on account of her being Jewish.[74] To suggest that Anne Frank is a universal symbol for suffering, or even the deaths of children killed in war and conflict is to de-Judaise the Holocaust.

Universalisation, Americanisation or globalisation?

Although this chapter has explored the relevance and implications of Holocaust universalisation on education, it is important to acknowledge that some scholars such as Bialystok,[75] Berenbaum and Kramer,[76] Rosenfeld[77] and Flanzbaum[78] have specifically emphasised the Americanisation of the Holocaust, although the term has often been used in different ways. Discussions have especially revolved around popular culture and memory, with two of the most contentious issues relating to the diary of Anne Frank and the establishing of the United States Holocaust Memorial Museum in Washington DC. While Americanisation and universalisation are undoubtedly connected, they

DOI: 10.1057/9781137388575.0008

are not the same thing, although many of the implications for the latter, such as de-Judaisation, have also been applied to the former.

Macgilchrist and Christophe, rather than talking about universalisation per se, refer to the impact of globalisation on Holocaust education. They emphasise among other things:

> A number of transnational or international actors, from non-governmental organizations such as the Task Force for International Cooperation on Holocaust Education, Remembrance and Research (ITF) to supranational bodies such as the OSCE's Office for Democratic Institutions and Human Rights (ODIHR) or the Council of Europe, which try to influence national teaching practice by offering (non-binding) guidelines or (binding) directives.[79]

They also discuss the importance of private corporations which acquire 'ownership rights in different local textbook markets',[80] arguing that though both fill 'global relevancy spaces', they can actually lead to diversification and heterogeneous outcomes in different national and local contexts.

Although debates concerning the Americanisation and globalisation of the Holocaust do have their own identity within the Holocaust studies, they are indubitably connected to the dichotomy between Holocaust particularism and universalism. In his thoughtful essay, 'The Holocaust and Jewish Identity in America: Memory, the Unique and the Universal', Magid suggests that what is perhaps required is 'a deft combination of universalizing and meaning without erasing the particularistic nature of the event in question'.[81] Understanding how such a dualistic approach is to work in practice is one of the greatest challenges which the memory and education of the Holocaust appears to face. As the Holocaust increasingly evolves as a universal cultural and moral symbol, maintaining historical specificity and context is going to become even harder. These are issues which have already become important parts of Holocaust education.

Notes

1   Hartman, G. (2009) 'Foreword', in Alexander, J. C. (Ed.) *Remembering the Holocaust: A Debate*, (Oxford: Oxford University Press), p. ix.

2   Alexander, J. C. (2002) 'On the Social Construction of Moral Universals: The "Holocaust" from War Crime to Trauma Drama', *European Journal of Social Theory*, 5: 1, 5–85, p. 52.

DOI: 10.1057/9781137388575.0008

3   Alexander, 'On the Social Construction', p. 52.

4   Levy, D. and Sznaider, N. (2002) 'Memory Unbound: The Holocaust and the Formation of Cosmopolitan Memory', *European Journal of Social Theory*, 5: 1, 87–106, p. 88.

5   Hirsch, M. and Spitzer, L. (2009) 'The Witness in the Archive: Holocaust Studies/Memory Studies', *Memory Studies*, 2: 2, 151–170, p. 164.

6   Pearce, A. (2014) *Holocaust Consciousness in Contemporary Britain*, (Abingdon: Routledge).

7   Yablonka, H. (2003) 'The Development of Holocaust Consciousness in Israel: The Nuremberg, Kapos, Kastner and Eichmann Trials', *Israel Studies*, 8: 3, 1–24.

8   Moses, A. D. (2003) 'Genocide and Holocaust Consciousness in Australia', *History Compass*, 1: 1, 1–11.

9   Caldwell, J. (2011) *Holocaust Consciousness in New Zealand 1980-2010: A Study.* Unpublished MA Thesis, Victoria University, Wellington, p. 116.

10   Magilov, D. (2007) 'Counting to Six Million: Collecting Projects and Holocaust Memorialization', *Jewish Social Studies*, 14: 1, 23–39, p. 23.

11   USHMM and Salzburg Global Seminar, (2013) *Global Perspectives on Holocaust Education: Trends, Patterns and Practices* (Working Draft), (Washington DC: USHMM), p. 29.

12   Schweber, S. (2006) 'Holocaust Fatigue', *Social Education*, 7: 1, 44–50, p. 48.

13   Salmons, P. (2001) 'Moral Dilemmas: History Teaching and the Holocaust', *Teaching History*, 104, 34–40, p. 38.

14   Schweber, 'Holocaust Fatigue', p. 48.

15   Magilov, 'Collecting Projects', p. 25.

16   Maginov, 'Collecting Projects', p. 36.

17   Salmons, P. (2010) 'Universal Meaning or Historical Understanding: The Holocaust in History and History in the Curriculum', *Teaching History*, 141, 57–63, p. 58.

18   Frank, M. (2013) 'The Holocaust Taken in Vain to Promote Gun Rights', Available: http:www.theguardian.com Accessed 3 September 2013.

19   'Pope likens Abortion to Holocaust', Available: http://www.bbc.co.uk Accessed 3 September 2013.

20   Available: http://www.peta.org Accessed 3 September 2013.

21   'High Court Rules against PETA Holocaust ad Campaign', Available: http://www.thelocal.de Accessed 3 September 2013.

22   Cohen, E. (2013) *Identity and Pedagogy: Shoah Education in Israeli State Schools*, (Brighton, MA: Academic Studies Press), p. 23.

23   Bearing Witness Evermore, 24 August 2013. Available: http://www.economist.com Accessed 3 September 2013.

24   Rabbi B. Block. Available: http://www.rabbiblock.com Accessed 3 September 2013.

DOI: 10.1057/9781137388575.0008

25   Solomon, A. (2011) *The Paradox of Holocaust Humour: Comedy that Illuminates Tragedy*, (New York: Proquest, Umi Dissertation Publishing, City University of New York), Abstract.

26   Ostrower, C. (2000) *Humour as a Defence Mechanism in the Holocaust.* Unpublished PhD Thesis, Tel-Aviv University.

27   Richardson, Alasdair. (2012) *Holocaust Education: An Investigation into the Types of Learning that Take Place when Students Encounter the Holocaust.* Unpublished EdD Thesis, Brunel University, p. 116.

28   Bauer, Y. (1994) 'Conclusion: The Significance of the Final Solution', in Cesarani, D. (Ed.) *The Final Solution: Origins and Implementation*, (London: Routledge), p. 306.

29   Bearing Witness Evermore, 24 August 2013. Available: http://www.economist.com Accessed 3 September 2013.

30   Richardson, Anna. (2005) 'The Ethical Limitations of Holocaust Literacy Representation', *eSharp*, 5 (University of Glasgow), p. 1.

31   Salmons, P. (2012) *Holocaust Memorial Day: How Secure is Holocaust Memory?* Huffington Post (27 January 2012).

32   Haggith, T. and Newman, J. (2005) 'Introduction', in Haggith, T. and Newman, J. (Eds) *Holocaust and the Moving Image: Representations in Film and Television since 1933*, (London: Wallflower Press), p. 8.

33   Doneson, J. (2002) 'Introduction', in Doneson, J. (Ed.) *The Holocaust in American Film*, (New York: Syracuse University Press), 1–12, p. 5.

34   Riley, K., Washington, E. and Humphries, E. (2011) 'Facing History and Ourselves: Noble Purpose, Unending Controversy', in Totten, S. and Pedersen, J. (Eds) *Teaching and Studying Social Issues: Major Programs and Approaches*, (Charlotte, North Carolina: Information Age Publishing), pp. 119–139, p. 121.

35   Riley, Washington and Humphries, 'Facing History and Ourselves', p. 122.

36   Gold, T., Kennedy, R., Levi, T. and Reiss, F. (2005) 'The Survivors Right to Reply', in Haggith, T. and Newman, J. (Eds) *Holocaust and the Moving Image: Representations in Film and Television since 1933*, (London: Wallflower Press), p. 248.

37   Gold et al., *The Survivors Right to Reply*, p. 248.

38   Gray, M. (2013) 'The Boy in the Striped Pyjamas: A Blessing or Curse for Holocaust Educators?' Paper presented at *The Future of Holocaust Studies Conference*, Universities of Southampton and Winchester, 29–31 July 2013.

39   Gray, 'The Boy in the Striped Pyjamas', p. 3.

40   Gray, 'The Boy in the Striped Pyjamas', p. 5.

41   Gray, 'The Boy in the Striped Pyjamas', p. 5.

42   Gray, 'The Boy in the Striped Pyjamas', p. 3.

43   USHMM, *Global Trends*, p. 18.

44   USHMM, *Global Trends*, p. 31.

DOI: 10.1057/9781137388575.0008

45 Fallace, T. (2008) *The Emergence of Holocaust Education in American Schools*, (New York: Palgrave Macmillan).

46 Santerini, M. (2003) 'Holocaust Education in Italy', *Intercultural Education*, 14: 2, 225–232, p. 227.

47 Santerini, 'Holocaust Education', p. 226.

48 Pettigrew, A., Foster, S., Howson, J., Salmons, P., Lenga, R- A. and Andrews, K. (2009) *Teaching about the Holocaust in English Secondary Schools: An Empirical Study of National Trends, Perspectives and Practice*, (Holocaust Education Development Programme, Institute of Education, University of London), p. 43.

49 McIntyre, M. (2008) 'To What Extent and in What Ways Does a Facing History and Ourselves Course on Holocaust and Human Behaviour Impact Students' Knowledge of and Attitudes towards the Holocaust?' MA Education (History and Citizenship), Institute of Education, University of London, Unpublished MA Thesis, p. 88.

50 Morgan, P. (2010) 'How Can We Deepen and Broaden Post-16 Students' Historical Engagement with the Holocaust? Developing a Rationale and Methods for Using Film', *Teaching History*, 141, 27–32, p. 27.

51 Rensmann, L. (2005) *Holocaust Education in Germany: An Interview*. PBS Frontline (19 May 2005).

52 Stevick, D. and Michaels, D. (2013) 'Empirical and Normative Foundations of Holocaust Education: Bringing Research and Advocacy into Dialogue', *Intercultural Education*, 24: 1–2, 1–18, p. 14.

53 Cole, T. (2000) *Selling the Holocaust*, (New York: Routledge), p. 42.

54 Bauer, Y. (2001) *Re-thinking the Holocaust*, (New Haven: Yale University Press), p. 23.

55 Balberg, E. (1999) *The Impact of the Holocaust Literature and Film*. Paper presented at Yad Vashem, 14 October 1999.

56 Pettigrew et al., *Teaching about the Holocaust*, p. 31.

57 Pettigrew et al., *Teaching about the Holocaust*, p. 49.

58 Lange, A. (2008) *A Survey of Teachers' Experiences and Perceptions in Relation to Teaching about the Holocaust*, (Stockholm: Living History Forum), p. 60.

59 Short, G. (2003) 'Lessons of the Holocaust: A Response to the Critics', *Educational Review*, 55: 3, 277–287, p. 285.

60 Eckmann, M. (2010) 'Exploring the Relevance of Holocaust Education for Human Rights Education', *Prospects* 40: 1, 7–16, p. 10.

61 Task Force for International Cooperation, Holocaust Education, Remembrance and Research, (2010) 'Educational Working Group Paper on the Holocaust and Other Genocides', p. 5.

62 Riley, Washington and Humphries, 'Facing History and Ourselves'.

63 Hondius, D. (2010) 'Finding Common Good in Education about the Holocaust and Slavery', *Intercultural Education*, 21: S1, S61–S69, pp. S62–S63.

64   Hondius, 'Finding Common Ground', p. S68.

65   Salmons, 'Universal Meaning ... ?', p. 61.

66   Bialystok, F. (1996) 'Americanizing the Holocaust: Beyond the Limit of the Universal', in Millen, R.L. (Ed.) *New Perspectives on the Holocaust*, (New York and London: New York University Press), p. 127.

67   Salmons, 'Universal Meaning ... ?', p. 58.

68   Fallace, T. (2008) *The Emergence of Holocaust Education in American Schools*, (New York: Palgrave Macmillan), p. 181.

69   Nates, T. (2010) ' "But, Apartheid Was Also Genocide ... What about Our Suffering?" Teaching the Holocaust in South Africa – Opportunities and Challenges', *Intercultural Education*, 21: S1, S17–S26, p. S17.

70   Gerstenfeld, M. (2009) *The Abuse of Holocaust Memory: Distortions and Responses*, (Jerusalem: Jerusalem Center for Public Affairs), p. 79.

71   Gerstenfeld, *The Abuse of Holocaust Memory*, p. 79.

72   Gerstenfeld, *The Abuse of Holocaust Memory*, p. 79.

73   Barnouw, D. (1998) *Anne Frank: Voor Beginners en Gevorderden*, (Den Haag: Sdu), p. 37.

74   See Salmons, 'Universal Meaning ... ?', p. 59.

75   Bialystok, 'Americanizing the Holocaust', p. 127.

76   Berenbaum, M. and Kramer, A. (1993) *The World Must Know: The History of the Holocaust as Told in the United States Holocaust Memorial Museum*, (Washington DC: USHMM).

77   Rosenfeld, A. (1995) 'The Americanization of the Holocaust', *Commentary*, 99: 6, 35–41.

78   Flanz, H. (Ed.) (1999) *The Americanization of the Holocaust*, (Maryland: The John Hopkins University Press).

79   Macgilchrist, F. and Christophe, B. (2011) 'Translating Globalization Theories into Educational Research: Thoughts on Recent Shifts in Holocaust Education', *Discourse: Studies in the Cultural Politics of Education*, 32: 1, 145–158, p. 148.

80   Macgilchrist and Christophe, 'Discourse', p. 149.

81   Magid, S. (2012) 'The Holocaust and Jewish Identity in America: Memory, the Unique, and the Universal', *Jewish Social Studies: History, Culture, Society*, 18: 2, 100–135, p. 124.

DOI: 10.1057/9781137388575.0008

5
Teaching the Holocaust without Survivors

Abstract: *The eventual absence of Holocaust survivors poses a number of challenges for Holocaust education. In addition to highlighting some of these issues, the means of addressing them are analysed, including video testimonies, making use of the second and third generation and integrating survivor accounts into Holocaust programmes of study. The dependence on survivor testimonies as a pedagogic tool is also called into question with a discussion of the educational opportunities which are opened up by the post-survivor era. This particularly includes a greater use of perpetrator testimonies.*

Keywords: perpetrator; survivor accounts; testimony; video testimony

Gray, Michael. *Contemporary Debates in Holocaust Education.* Basingstoke: Palgrave Macmillan, 2014. DOI: 10.1057/9781137388575.0009.

Across the globe, survivors have played a key role in Holocaust education, playing an important part in its development and delivery. According to the IHRA:

> First-person survivor testimony in many countries has been an integral part of Holocaust education since its inception. They have been, and continue to be, the bearers of witness in educational frameworks, both formal and informal, in classrooms, museums, and on student visits to memorial sites.[1]

The JESNA report of 2006 stated that the primary educational benefits of survivor presentations include, 'the immediacy of first-hand experience to convey the reality of the Holocaust, the possibility of personal interaction with Holocaust survivors [and] the emotional power and connection with individuals who experienced the Holocaust.'[2] It is impossible to know the total number of students around the world who have heard survivor testimonies over the years or the full impact that it has had upon their knowledge, understanding and outlooks, yet as Maio, Traum and Debevec note, 'for more than 60 years, Holocaust survivors have recounted their stories thousands of times to thousands of children all over the world, giving insights and without a doubt changing the perspective of those children for the rest of their lives'.[3]

Yet the reality is such that survivors will not be here forever. More than 20 years ago Schwartz wrote, 'the number of survivors are dwindling and their greatest fear is that with their passing the memory and lessons of the Holocaust will be lost to succeeding generation.'[4] Since then important initiatives and measures have been put in place to preserve memory, yet the integral role that survivors play in Holocaust education means that educators and scholars have been forced to consider the nature of Holocaust education in a post-survivor world. This naturally poses challenges, but also opportunities to reconsider and adapt the means and methods whereby the Holocaust is taught.

The place of survivors within Holocaust education has evolved over the years.[5] In the immediate post-war period, the absence of Holocaust consciousness and of specific Holocaust education meant that Jewish survivor tales were viewed merely as a part of general stories which emerged from the Second World War. As survivor testimonies, most notably those published by Primo Levi and Elie Wiesel, became increasingly popular, the demand for survivors to play an active role in Holocaust education increased. Survivor involvement in education particularly increased throughout the late 1980s and 1990s. This surge emerged as a consequence

DOI: 10.1057/9781137388575.0009

of many survivors reaching retirement age and thus being freer to speak in schools during the day, the significant impact of *Schindler's List* and the increased awareness that the first-hand accounts of survivors would only be available for a limited period of time. In recent years, the demand for survivors to visit schools and to share their stories has continued unabated. In Canada, survivors connected to the Montreal Holocaust Memorial Centre spoke to nearly 13,000 people during 2011–2012 with approximately half of these testimonies being given in schools.[6] In the UK, Holocaust survivor visits are almost typically arranged through the Holocaust Educational Trust (HET), and the number of visits during the academic year 2012–2013 actually increased from 383 in the previous year to 504. Out of this figure, over 90 per cent (n. 456) of the visits were made to schools, with the others taking place in universities, pupil referral units, synagogues, family centres, churches and other institutions. Despite the increasing age and frailty of many survivors, it is very seldom indeed for the Trust to be unable to accommodate requests for speakers with those rare occasions typically occurring due to the geographical location of the institution which makes travel for the survivor very long and difficult. Perhaps surprisingly, the number of survivors who shared their testimony through the Trust during 2012–2013 increased by almost 31 per cent on the previous year, some of whom had never previously testified their experiences. This suggests the desire, or perhaps obligation, to share their stories, memories and accounts before it is too late. Yet it is inevitable that in the not-too-distant future the demand for Holocaust survivor visits will irreversibly exceed supply.

Such demand continues to be relatively high at present. In his major study of Holocaust education in Israel, Cohen found that 'by 9th grade...70% [of students] had heard testimonies of survivors either in person or on videotape'.[7] In the work of the HEDP in England, 25 per cent of respondents (n. 248) said that they were likely to invite a Holocaust survivor into school, while 60 per cent (n. 564) suggested that they were unlikely to do so. Despite this, teachers observed that survivor stories played an important role in their teaching of the Holocaust with 78 teachers out of 1,187 stating that survivor testimonies were their most useful and effective resource.[8] It is often on the occasion of a national day of Holocaust remembrance that survivor visits to schools are particularly in demand, and according to the ODIHR report on education on the Holocaust, they play a particularly important role in the national remembrance of Romania, Luxembourg and Bulgaria, while throughout

DOI: 10.1057/9781137388575.0009

the year in Austria 'through its in-service training for teachers, the state assists schools in inviting witnesses, survivors, and victims of National Socialism to lead lectures and discussions'.[9]

Many scholars see the use of testimony as a central part of sound Holocaust pedagogy. Dreier states for example that 'dealing with Holocaust and survivors' testimonies should be part of regular teaching',[10] although there is legitimacy in asking why this ought to be. The arguments for doing so are manifold and include among the most important the opportunity to rehumanise the victim. In addition to this, individual stories help develop understanding of what the Holocaust meant at personal level amidst what Magen calls 'a cluster of accessible and tangible human stories'.[11] In addition to this, many see the testimonies of Holocaust survivors as providing greater relevance to pupils, bringing the subject alive, as it were, and helping to provide context to the history. Listening to survivor testimonies has also been viewed as an important means of bearing witness, or at least being witnesses to the witnesses. Yet complexities and divergence of opinion abound when dealing with the survivor testimonies as Rothberg and Stark demonstrate by asking the following questions:

> What does it mean to attempt to record and preserve such testimony? How do such images affect our understanding of the past and our relation to the future? What is the role of the survivor's voice and image in shaping Holocaust history and memory?[12]

It is these questions, in specific relation to Holocaust education, which this chapter attempts to explore.

Preserving memories

For over 30 years, there have been methodical and meticulous efforts to preserve the memories and the testimonies of survivors after their deaths for the education and enlightenment of future generations. Andrews writes that:

> For many of us working in the area of Holocaust education around the globe, one question has been raised repeatedly over the past years: How do we ensure that the survivor voice continues to be heard when individuals are no longer able to tell their stories?[13]

The predominant means of doing this has been through video recordings of survivors' stories. In 1979, the Fortunoff Video Archive was

DOI: 10.1057/9781137388575.0009

established at Yale University and now houses over 4,200 testimonies, which is over 10,000 hours of video footage.[14] McGill University's 'Living Testimonies Project' has more than 100 survivor interviews, while the Montreal Holocaust Memorial Centre's 'Testimony Project' has recorded over 450 accounts.[15] By far the largest collection of survivor testimonies is the USC Shoah Foundation Institute for Visual History and Education, which was originally established by Steven Spielberg in 1994 as the Survivors of the Shoah Visual History Foundation. The archive now holds the testimonies of nearly 52,000 survivors and other witnesses, from 57 countries in 33 languages. It would take over 12 years to watch every person's account as the archive consists of over 100,000 hours of footage.[16] Although the entire archive is available at 44 institutions around the world, its use in the classroom revolves around the IWitness programme, which has a more manageable 1,300 testimonies and is discussed in detail in Chapter 6.

Most of the testimonies in these archives have been criticised because they were recorded in the 1980s and 1990s. Questions have been asked as to whether survivors can really remember such detail so many decades after the event. Browning, writing of his experiences using both earlier and later testimonies highlights an important advantage of these later accounts when he states:

> Survivors giving very late testimonies in the 1990s were able to broach previously taboo subjects – such as revenge killings among Jewish prisoners – for the first time; I discovered that 'late' testimonies given 50 or 60 years after the events could not be summarily dismissed in favor of exclusive reliance on 'early' testimonies.[17]

In addition to disputes concerning their validity, there also continues to be a lack of consensus about the pedagogic value of video testimonies and for some they appear to be inadequate attempts at replacing survivors in the classroom. Polak observes that, 'teachers often feel that to invite an eyewitness into the classroom is "the real thing" and using video testimony is second best and therefore not considered, even when inviting someone in person is not viable.'[18] By contrast, Herscovitch suggests that comparisons between the two ought not to exist.

> The stated expectation often heard is that recorded testimony will replace survivor in-class or live testimony. They cannot be equated. It is up to educational institutions to use video testimony, as well as archival documents and artefacts to relate the human story of the Holocaust.[19]

DOI: 10.1057/9781137388575.0009

This sharp distinction which Herscovitch advocates between real-life survivor testimonies and video recordings seems somewhat contradicted by the empirical research of Beaver. Based on his study of 75 pupils' experiences of watching over 100 hours of testimony from more than 300 Holocaust survivors and witnesses, Beaver noted:

> Analysis of students' comments reveals the emotional and personal con-
> nections expressed in response to watching testimony. Students continually
> described the experience of watching video testimony by using words and
> phrases like 'personal,' 'feel their emotion,' 'feel like I know the Holocaust
> survivor,' and 'people I met.' As one student noted…'it goes past the com-
> puter screen and feels like she [survivor] is actually telling her story directly
> to me.'[20]

Beaver not only pointed to the increase in knowledge that students who watched video testimonies acquired compared with the control but also argued that 'potential cognitive gains from using video testimony in the classroom are significant, and merit further investigation and validation with a larger student population.'[21] The potential of Holocaust video testi-mony is also assessed by Clark in specific relation to tackling apathy and indifference, drawing on the relationship that Holocaust testimony has with oral history among other things.[22] Street raises the valuable point that such testimonies are not to be viewed in a vacuum. She notes that 'in order to work with audio-visual testimony effectively and ethically, it is imperative that one understands the content's historical context and specific detail.'[23]

Yet video archives of Holocaust testimonies are not the only means of sharing the experiences of survivors within the classrooms of the future. One way whereby students can have first-hand experiences is through listening to the testimonies of survivors' children, who share the stories and accounts which were previously told by their parent or grandparents. 'Next Generations' is an organisation in Florida, for example, made up of children and grandchildren of Holocaust survivors who seek to educate the future generations by 'preserving the memories of the past' including specifically working with schools and educators.[24] The 2006 report by JESNA stated that presentations by second-generation survivors can be very effective, particularly if combined with other speakers and materi-als, although it was also recognised that 'the second generation speaker is notably different from the first generation speaker and educators must consider how best to use them as resources.'[25]

DOI: 10.1057/9781137388575.0009

By experiencing the testimonies of the second generation, adolescents might not be seeing a survivor in the flesh, but can understand that had the survivor not lived through the Holocaust then the person testifying would not be present either. There are of course limitations to second and third generational testimonies. It seems unlikely that they will be able to answer every question which is posed or be able to talk about the emotions and feelings with the same levels of pathos, while in some cases survivors have chosen not to share their experiences with their children. Zembrzycki and High, in their study of survivors in Montreal, noted that 'one of the things that we found most surprising in our interviews with survivor-speakers was that a substantial number of them have chosen not to share their wartime experiences with friends and family.'[26]

Nevertheless, it could be argued that the testimonies of survivors' children and grandchildren, give an insight into something which is often lacking in first-hand survivor testimonies or those recorded for video archives. According to Kangisser Cohen, who based her findings on the life stories of 50 Holocaust survivors in Israel and Australia, most survivors do not discuss their family life or their children when sharing their testimonies and experiences.[27] Moreover, when testifying in schools, the limitations on time also often mean that there is minimal discussion of pre-war or post-war life. Ecker suggests that when teaching the Holocaust through testimony, the whole life story ought to be covered, although 'due to time restrictions it is usually not possible.'[28] Zembrzycki and High write that the majority of survivors 'tend to be most comfortable telling a chronological narrative that begins and ends with the violence.'[29] Conversely, those sharing their parents' stories are more likely to also include something of their own upbringing, the post-war experiences of the survivors and provide greater insight into their family relations. This is an important and valuable addition which may help students to contextualise and personalise the survivor's experiences. Herscovitch summarises this when she states:

> Oral-history collections offer a breadth of experiences, tell stories of life before the Holocaust, and promote understanding regarding the diversity of Jewish life and experience. They also underscore the importance of understanding antisemitism as a historical phenomenon, and help humanize, contemporize, and universalize understanding of the Holocaust.[30]

Similarly, Martin, in her article on how to 'draw students in' when teaching about the Holocaust, recommends getting 'volunteers to make

DOI: 10.1057/9781137388575.0009

classroom presentations on Holocaust survivors personally known to them'.[31] She admittedly recognises that this may not be easy in some institutions and that it is not a pedagogic method which is going to be available in the future. Nevertheless, Martin states:

> There is nothing abstract or dry about hearing friends or acquaintances tell about the ordeals or deaths of their own grandparents, great-aunts, and cousins. I have learned that, although students cannot fairly be presumed to care about things they don't know much about, if you give them a chance to find out how real people were affected by a historical event, you will often find that they can care very much indeed.[32]

Although the evidence put forward is based solely on personal experience, if true, the method advocated by Martin could be adapted to fit into a post-survivor era. While students may not be able to talk to the survivors themselves in preparation for their presentations, they can speak to those members of their family who knew the survivor and present the oral history which has been shared. Such a method helps to preserve and disseminate the accounts of the past and face the challenges of the post-survivor era.

Of course the Holocaust is by no means the first historical phenomenon to have to deal with the challenges which will emerge when the last survivor has deceased. While the same might be said of slavery, the emancipation of the serfs in Russia or the American Civil War, it is perhaps the loss of survivors from the First World War which is most comparable with the eventual absence of Holocaust survivors. Both the First World War and the Holocaust were watershed moments and those who survived were witnesses to a horror which has become memorialised and an important part of contemporary education. Students from around the world both remember and learn about the First World War through visiting historical sites such as battlefields, cemeteries and memorials like the Menin Gate in Ypres. In a similar way, the memory and education of the Holocaust also involves visiting historical sites such as concentration camps, former ghettos and memorials.

Yet in recent years, less orthodox means of educating about the First World War have been employed. The official archives of the UK government, for example, using its personal service records of one particular soldier, namely Private Henry Fairhurst of a Pals Battalion, offers videoconferencing sessions with schools whereby this particular soldier is played by a costumed actor, standing in a constructed trench. The actor answers the questions which are asked of him by the students as though

DOI: 10.1057/9781137388575.0009

he were Private Henry Fairhurst himself, using his detailed knowledge of the documents as the basis for his responses. A similar videoconference session is offered whereby a costumed actor plays the character of Olaudah Equiano, the eighteenth-century slave who bought his freedom and became a campaigner for abolition. Such video conference sessions are certainly one way of preserving testimony, although it raises various pedagogic and ethical dilemmas. After all, an actor can never really know how the historical figure would have answered the question and may thus lead to responses which are simply generalised statements about conditions and experiences. The National Archives in the UK do not have any intention of using costumed actors to answer questions about life in a ghetto or in a concentration camp, although this is no guarantee that such methods will not be employed by other organisations at some point in the future.

Perhaps a more effective way of combining testimony and documents is employed by the Centre for Holocaust Education (CfHE) in London, whose professional development programme uses amongst others the account of British Holocaust survivor Leon Greenman. Andrews writes that 'Leon's [video] testimony is given additional context through documents, photographs, and news reports relating to the events that he experienced personally in the year after he was liberated.'[33] This multimodal approach was because research had demonstrated the absence of teaching about pre-war Jewish life. The programme also explores survivors' post-war experiences which have also often been marginalised within the classroom.

Criticisms of survivor testimonies

The various programmes, archives and initiatives to preserve the voice of the survivor in the classroom all work on the belief that Holocaust education ought to make use of testimonies. While few would argue for the wholesale abandonment of survivor voices in the classroom, they undoubtedly pose difficulties and problems, both historically and pedagogically. Perhaps the most obvious and important point is that every Holocaust survivor is by definition untypical. For those who successfully lived out the war, survived the selection processes, the murderous work programmes or the death marches, there were countless others – the vast majority – who did not. Consequently, the testimonies that survivors

DOI: 10.1057/9781137388575.0009

tell are the exception, for what was most common was the prevention of any opportunity to testify. Blutinger states, 'a student who follows the journey and suffering of a survivor thus will get a distorted view of the Holocaust, since he or she will be reading the story of an exceptional case.'[34] One might go as far as Anna Richardson and say, 'survivor testimony can never express the full Holocaust experience, as by definition those who survived did not go to the gas chamber.'[35]

In addition to being untypical, another criticism of first-hand testimonies within Holocaust education is that some survivors tend to omit the most sensitive, traumatic or extreme incidents which they experienced or witnessed. Zembrzycki and High found specific examples of this in their research.

> Rena Schondorf, for instance, is always concerned about the effect that her story might have on children. To this end, she refrains from telling graphic and violent parts of her story when she speaks to those under the age of twelve. Even with adolescents, Rena spends little time recounting 'the different kind of hell' she experienced...When we asked Sidney Zoltak about the parts that he leaves out of his story, he told us that he omits any memories that he knows will trigger a strong emotional reaction.

In Alasdair Richardson's qualitative study, he found that after listening to one survivor, some students were surprised that the Holocaust had not been as bad as they had previously thought.[36] It seems that many adolescents lack the knowledge to recognise the huge range of circumstances that were witnessed by survivors and the variation which existed across Europe. Consequently, survivor testimonies in the classroom may inadvertently lead students into thinking that everyone who encountered the Holocaust had a relatively uniform set of experiences. Richardson also suggests, in line with the findings of Clements,[37] that survivors in the classroom disempowered teachers by replacing them as the predominant source of expertise, which might damage the future learning of students in their continuation of Holocaust education.[38]

Clearly one of the most problematic aspects of using survivor testimony, which has been frequently raised by scholars, is relating to memory. How many of the details can a survivor really remember and to what extent have post-war accounts been influenced by external sources? Blutinger writes, 'Survivor testimony...raises questions of reliability and accuracy. Over time, the specifics of memory can fade and survivor accounts can be influenced by later experiences, images, and

DOI: 10.1057/9781137388575.0009

other testimony.'[39] Bartov, however, suggests that testimonies ought to be viewed in the same way that any other piece of evidence is considered.

> Clearly, testimonies do not tell a single story; they are full of contradictions, errors, misjudgments, and untruths – though no more than any other document. They should be treated with the same care and suspicion as any piece of evidence pulled out of an archive but also with the respect due every important piece of the puzzle of the past.[40]

Laub has challenged the sceptical attitude of many historians and by approaching the issue from a psychoanalytic angle has argued that the knowledge of the historian can prevent them from being able to recognise what can be learnt from such testimonies beyond that which is simply factual. She shifts the focus of the testimony away from historical accuracy and explores the importance of testimony from a multidisciplinary perspective.

> Testimony, as I describe it, does not have to adhere to the rules of evidence relevant to juridical testimony; it does not lay claim to historical factuality and to 'objectivity'; it is not intended to bring 'the News' to the public like a journalistic interview. It is rather a journey into the deepest recesses of oneself.[41]

Laub's position has been strongly criticised by the likes of Trezise and brings into discussion what testimony is ultimately all about.[42]

At the forefront of analysis on the use of survivor testimony is Browning's thoughtful and balanced arguments in his book *Collected Memories: Holocaust History and Postwar Testimony*. He advocates the use of such testimonies, but within the confines of a critical methodology which would typically be applied to evidence.

> The use of survivor testimony, therefore, is not a Holocaust historian's 'silver bullet' that will answer all his questions and solve all his problems. Claiming that survivor testimony must be accorded a privileged position, not subject to the same critical analysis and rules of evidence as other sources, or, even worse, lodging the indiscriminate accusation that a historian has not used survivor testimony as a weapon to discredit both his or her work and character, will not serve the cause of integrating survivor testimonies into the writing of Holocaust history.[43]

Since then, Friedländer in his masterpiece, *The Years of Extermination*, has demonstrated the art of writing an integrated history, which thoughtfully and judiciously employs the voices of survivors in telling the story of

DOI: 10.1057/9781137388575.0009

the Holocaust.[44] Bartov too advocates 'the integration of testimonies into the historical reconstruction of the Holocaust as documents of validity equal to that of other forms of documentation'.[45] In many senses, it is this difficult integrated approach which is also needed in the classroom.

Supportive of this is the groundbreaking work of Greenspan, who innovatively suggests that rather than moving away from testimony one must go beyond it. By this he is specifically referring to the way survivors pass on their knowledge, understanding and experiences so that there is a dialogue rather than a monologue.[46] Through frequent discussions with survivors over many years, Greenspan found that the complexities of the experiences had become easier to understand. He thus challenges the terminology and methodology of working with survivors, principally advocating sustained conversation and collaboration between the survivor and the other person in the dialogue. While it is by and large too late to implement such a methodology on Holocaust survivors, it has already been put into use with survivors of other genocides.

Greenspan's approach seems compatible with the critical methodology advocated by Browning and seems to challenge the almost unquestioning nature of Holocaust video testimonies which are used in the classroom. Clearly, a universally trusting approach to the accounts of the Holocaust survivor is highly problematic, as Byford shows in his examination of post-war testimonies in socialist Yugoslavia.[47]

As far as using Holocaust testimony within education goes, it seems that a balanced and moderated approach is needed. Testimonies provide an invaluable source of understanding and may be particularly useful in confronting many of the issues raised within religious education and citizenship programmes. Within the teaching of history, testimonies, be they in the form of videos or text, provide an insight into the Holocaust, which are neither infallible nor useless.

Perpetrator testimonies

If methodological rigour and care are needed in the selection and evaluation of survivor testimonies, the same can certainly be said of perpetrator testimonies. With the eventual cessation of Holocaust survivor visits to the classroom, there have been suggestions that this provides a valuable opportunity to put greater emphasis on the voice of the perpetrator, which to date has been largely marginalised within Holocaust education.

DOI: 10.1057/9781137388575.0009

With limited curriculum time, it is more often than not that the account of the survivor is heard within the classroom and in the museums, often through first-person testimonies. The availability of documentation and evidence, generated by those who implemented the killing, may gradually fill at least some of the gap which has been created by the passing of the survivor generation. This poses both a number of important opportunities and challenges.

Perhaps one of the most valuable prospects is an increased focus on why the Holocaust occurred. While survivor testimonies have been crucial in helping to answer questions such as 'what?', 'when?' and 'how?', they are limited in their ability to explain 'why?'. To answer this, it is the testimony of the perpetrator which is needed. It is typically a different set of questions and outcomes which are being asked and pursued through the use of perpetrator testimonies. In his examination of the Eichmann testimony, for example, Browning asks, 'which parts, if any, can be deemed possibly or even probably accurate and reliable, and what, if anything, do they tell us about the decisions for the Final Solution?'[48] It is questions such as these which need to be employed through the use of perpetrator testimony within Holocaust education.

Using the accounts of perpetrators is likely to include studying post-war accounts, either generated by interviews or by the various court cases which have been held around the world. In some instances, students can study such discourse alongside documentation and evidence from the time of the Holocaust. As part of his work for the film *Shoah*, Lanzmann secretly filmed two former members of the Einsatzgruppen for example. In the case of Karl Kretschmer, who was Obersturmführer with Einsatzgruppe 4a, which was responsible for the massacre at Babi Yar, students may wish to explore Lanzmann's interview while simultaneously analysing a letter that Kretschmer wrote to his family in September 1942 about Babi Yar. Vice argues that these clandestine interviews are of great value in many ways although she predominantly focuses her argument on the 'filmic representation of mass murder and its effects on the perpetrators'.[49] Nevertheless, in her paper 'Holocaust Perpetrators in Teaching and Research', Vice does raise some valuable questions about the suitability of such testimonies, asking whether perpetrator testimony might make 'ordinary men' unordinary and whether or not it creates an emotional distance between testator and pupil?[50]

Yet one of the potential key benefits of introducing perpetrator testimonies into the classroom is that rather than making them seem unordinary, it helps pupils to recognise that those who implemented the Holocaust were not universally deranged or psychotic. Schilling correctly states, 'while there were perpetrators who fit the demonic, psychologically disturbed image – one thinks, for example, of Kurt Franz, Treblinka's deputy commander – the empirical evidence does not support this characterization of most perpetrators.'[51] In his insightful examination of how best to use perpetrator testimonies within education, Schilling concludes that effective teaching is dependent upon 'moving beyond the dead end of demonizing while sustaining a creative tension between understanding and moral judgement.'[52] This concurs with Vice's suggestion that pedagogic suitability involves more than simply content.

Blutinger, like Vice, also advocates teaching 'the Holocaust both from a victim-centered perspective, as well as from a perpetrator-based perspective.'[53] He argues that this dualistic approach is 'essential in order to give the students a fuller understanding of the issues surrounding this event.'[54] Blutinger wisely warns of some of the dangers involved with teaching the Holocaust in a way that marginalises the lives and actions of the victims and focuses almost exclusively on the 'historical actors'. He writes, 'perpetrator-based discourse not only mirrors Nazi language, it exacerbates the image of Jews as going passively to their deaths like sheep to the slaughter.'[55]

Clearly, therefore, using perpetrator testimonies generates a wide range of important educational and ethical questions. Perhaps most problematic are post-war testimonies themselves, as some pupils may use such sources to deny or marginalise the nature or extent of the Holocaust or in some cases to fuel their existing prejudices. Moreover, there is a danger that adolescents may fall into the trap of believing the various testimonies without realising the motives of the perpetrators or the compelling evidence which stands against them. Similar challenges also exist when using within the classroom sources written by perpetrators. Pupils are unlikely to understand the euphemistic language and may not have the disciplinary tools to comprehend the messages which are being conveyed. While there may well be benefits for increasing the use of perpetrator testimonies in helping to understand the Holocaust, the selection of appropriate material and the way that it is used in the classroom must be considered thoughtfully and judiciously.

In his discussion of the use of perpetrator testimonies within Holocaust education, Levine suggests that the voice of the perpetrator is just as important as the survivor in the work of pedagogy. He argues

DOI: 10.1057/9781137388575.0009

that by shifting more of the focus onto perpetrator testimonies, it will help the teaching of the Holocaust to come away from a purely 'Jewish experience', which has, according to Levine, been one of the causes of Holocaust fatigue and disinterest among many European adolescents.[56] Magen too, when discussing the use of testimony, writes that 'it is proper to note the importance of learning about the human aspects of people in categories other than the Jews, such as rescuers, bystanders, collaborators, and perpetrators.'[57] Even if 'the Holocaust' as a term is defined as exclusively referring to Jews, then understanding the Holocaust nevertheless involves understanding the agency, actions, experiences and motivations of those who were involved in the Holocaust in a non-Jewish capacity. The possible overemphasis on survivor testimony has potentially marginalised the multifaceted and highly complex nature of the Holocaust and oversimplified complex concept terms such as victims, bystanders or perpetrators.

The future of survivor testimony in the classroom

It is difficult to say with confidence what future direction Holocaust education will take with regards to its use of survivor testimonies. Despite the eventual passing of those who witnessed and endured the horrors first-hand, it seems unlikely that their voices and stories will be forgotten or even marginalised. This is in no small part due to the commitment and willingness that survivors have demonstrated to share their experiences and due to organisations that have preserved them. It seems probable that central to the way that testimony use within the classroom evolves will be the simultaneous development of the technology which allows the accounts of survivors to be accessed, utilised and integrated into a programme of study. This is an ever-changing area but one which is likely to be of great significance in the future of Holocaust education.

Notes

1   Task Force for International Cooperation, Holocaust Education, Remembrance and Research. (2010) 'Educational Working Group Paper on Teaching the Holocaust without Survivors', p. 1.
2   Isaacs, L., Rosov, W., Raff, L., Rosenblatt, S., Hecht, S., Rozenek, M. and Rotem, Z. (2006) 'Best Practices in Holocaust Education': Report to the San

DOI: 10.1057/9781137388575.0009

Francisco Jewish Community Endowment Fund, Jewish Education Service of North America, p. 12.

3   Maio, H., Traum, D. and Debevec, P. (2012) 'New Dimensions in Testimony', *Past Forward*, Summer 2012, 22–26, p. 23.

4   Schwartz, D. (1990) ' "Who Will Tell Them after We're Gone?": Reflections on Teaching the Holocaust', *The History Teacher*, 23: 2, 95–110, p. 95.

5   Kushner, T. (2006) 'Holocaust Testimony, Ethics and the Problem of Representation', *Poetics Today*, 27: 2, 275–295.

6   Montreal Holocaust Memorial Centre. (2012) *Annual Report 2011–12*, p. 11.

7   Cohen, E. (2013) *Identity and Pedagogy: Shoah Education in Israeli State Schools*, (Brighton, MA: Academic Studies Press), p. 106.

8   Pettigrew, A., Foster, S., Howson, J., Salmons, P., Lenga, R- A. and Andrews, K. (2009) *Teaching about the Holocaust in English Secondary Schools: An Empirical Study of National Trends, Perspectives and Practice*, (Holocaust Education Development Programme, Institute of Education, University of London), pp. 44–45.

9   Office for Democratic Institutions and Human Rights. (2005) *Education on the Holocaust and on Anti-Semitism*, p. 46.

10 Dreier, W., Herscovitch, A. and Polak, K. (2013) 'A Slowly Escaping Landscape', *Past Forward*, Summer 2013, 32–34, p. 34.

11 Magen, S. (2012) 'Using Testimony in Holocaust Education', The International School for Holocaust Studies, Yad Vashem. Available: http://www.yadvashem.org Accessed 23 September 2013.

12 Rothberg, M. and Stark, J. (2003) 'After the Witness: A Report from the Twentieth Anniversary Conference of the Fortunoff Video Archive for Holocaust Testimonies at Yale', *History and Memory*, 15: 1, 85–96, p. 86.

13 Andrews, K. (2013) 'A Damned Good Cry', *Past Forward*, Summer 2013, 14–15, p. 14.

14 Rothberg and Stark, 'After the Witness'.

15 Zembrzycki, S. and High, S. (2012) 'When I was your Age': Bearing Witness in Holocaust Education in Montreal', *The Canadian Historical Review*, 93: 3, 408–435, p. 414.

16 Smith, S. (2013) 'Editorial', *Past Forward*, Summer 2013, 6, p. 6.

17 Browning, C. (2011) 'Remembering Survival', *Past Forward*, Spring 2011, 18–19, p. 19.

18 Dreier, Herscovitch and Polak, 'A Slowly Evolving Landscape', p. 33.

19 Dreier, Herscovitch and Polak, 'A Slowly Evolving Landscape', p. 33.

20 Beaver, C. (2013) 'IWitness Evaluation Report', *Past Forward*, Summer 2013, 30–32, p. 30.

21 Beaver, 'IWitness Evaluation Report', p. 30.

22 Clark, M. M. (2005) 'Holocaust Video Testimony, Oral History and Narrative Medicine: The Struggle against Indifference', *Literature and Medicine*, 24: 2, 266–282.

23 Street, K. (2013) 'Standing at the Intersection', *Past Forward*, Summer 2013, 16–17, p. 17.
24 http://www.nextgenerations.org
25 Isaacs et al., *Best Practices in Holocaust Education*, p. 14.
26 Zembrzycki and High, 'When I was your Age', p. 424.
27 Kangisser Cohen, S. (2010) 'Survivors of the Holocaust and Their Children', *Journal of Modern Jewish Studies*, 9: 2, 165–183.
28 IHRA, Educational Working Group Paper, 'Teaching the Holocaust without Survivors, p. 3.
29 Zembrzycki and High, 'When I was your Age', p. 421.
30 Dreier, Herscovitch and Polak, 'A Slowly Evolving Landscape', p. 34.
31 Martin, K. (2007) 'Teaching the Shoah: Four Approaches That Draw Students In', *The History Teacher*, 40: 4, 493–502, p. 495.
32 Martin, 'Teaching the Shoah', p. 495.
33 Andrews, 'A Damned Good Cry', pp. 14 15.
34 Blutinger, J. (2009) 'Bearing Witness: Teaching the Holocaust from a Victim-Centred Perspective', *The History Teacher*, 42: 3, 269–279, p. 274.
35 Richardson, Anna. (2005) 'The Ethical Limitations of Holocaust Literacy Representation', *eSharp*, 5 (University of Glasgow), p. 6.
36 Richardson, Alasdair. (2012) *Holocaust Education: An Investigation into the Types Of Learning That Take Place when Students Encounter the Holocaust.* Unpublished EdD Thesis, Brunel University, p. 122.
37 Clements, J. (2006) 'A Very Neutral Voice: Teaching about the Holocaust', *Educate*, 5: 1, 39–49.
38 Richardson, 'Holocaust Education', p. 126.
39 Blutinger, 'Bearing Witness', p. 275.
40 Bartov, O. (2011) 'Setting the Record Straight', *Past Forward*, Spring 2011, 24–26, p. 26.
41 Laub, D. (2009) 'On Holocaust Testimony and Its "Reception" within Its Own Frame, as a Process In Its Own Right: *A Response to "Between History and Psychoanalysis" by Thomas Trezise'*, *History and Memory*, 21: 1, 127–150, p. 142.
42 Trezise, T. (2008) 'Between History and Psychoanalysis: A Case Study in the Reception of Holocaust Survivor Testimony', *History and Memory*, 20: 1, 7–47.
43 Browning, C. (2003) *Collected Memories: Holocaust History and Postwar Testimony*, (London: University of Wisconsin Press), pp. 40–41.
44 Friedländer, S. (2007) *Nazi Germany and the Jews 1939–45: The Years of Extermination*, (New York: HarperCollins).
45 Bartov, 'Setting the Record Straight', p. 24.
46 Greenspan, H. (2010) *On Listening to Holocaust Survivors: Beyond Testimony*, (Minnesota: Paragon House) 2nd Ed.
47 Byford, J. (2010) '"Shortly Afterwards, We Heard the Sound of the Gas Van": Survivor Testimony and the Writing of History in Socialist Yugolslavia', *History and Memory*, 22: 1, 5–47.

DOI: 10.1057/9781137388575.0009

48   Browning, *Collected Memories*, p. 5.
49   Vice, S. (2011) 'Claude Lanzmann's Einsatzgruppen Interviews', *Holocaust Studies: A Journal of Culture and History*, 17: 2–3, 51–74, p. 51.
50   Vice, S. (2013) 'Holocaust Perpetrator in Teaching and Research', Paper presented at *The Future of Holocaust Studies Conference*, Universities of Southampton and Winchester, 29–31 July 2013.
51   Schilling, 'The Dead End of Demonizing', p. 198.
52   Schilling, D. (1996) 'The Dead End of Demonizing: Dealing with the Perpetrators in Teaching the Holocaust', in Millen, R. (Ed.) *New Perspectives on the Holocaust: A Guide for Teachers and Scholars*, (New York: New York University Press), p. 208.
53   Blutinger, 'Bearing Witness', pp. 269–270.
54   Blutinger, 'Bearing Witness', p. 270.
55   Blutinger, 'Bearing Witness', p. 269.
56   Levine, P. (2013) 'And After They Are Gone?' Paper presented at *The Future of Holocaust Studies Conference*, Universities of Southampton and Winchester, 29–31 July 2013.
57   Magen, S. (2012) 'Using Testimony in Holocaust Education'. Available: http://www.yadvashem.org Accessed 23 September 2013.

DOI: 10.1057/9781137388575.0009

6

The Digital Era of Holocaust Education

Abstract: *The rapid advances in technology provide a range of opportunities and challenges for Holocaust education. The pioneering research projects which are currently engaged in preserving interactive survivor testimonies for future generations and location-based learning are discussed along with their pedagogical implications. The use of the Holocaust within social media is critically analysed, with specific reference to memorialisation through Facebook and trivialisation through YouTube. The future of Holocaust learning is discussed in the light of existing advances with specific reference to web-based initiatives.*

Keywords: Facebook; online learning; smartphone; social media; technology; YouTube

Gray, Michael. *Contemporary Debates in Holocaust Education.* Basingstoke: Palgrave Macmillan, 2014. DOI: 10.1057/9781137388575.0010.

Whether or not developments in technology can benefit Holocaust education and help to tackle many of the challenges which it faces must be considered in the context of a wider debate. For many years there has been a lack of consensus regarding the value and purpose of new technology within the disciplines of teaching and learning. Hew and Brush are correct in stating that 'from the birth of the motion picture in 1922, to the advent of the computer in the mid-1970s, educators have been intrigued with the potential of technology to help transform education and improve student learning.'[1] Yet there are some, such as Daniel, who argue that technology has 'transformed all aspects of human life – except education' and that 'the continuing introduction of new technologies and new media has added little to the quality of most education.'[2] The studies in this area are by no means conclusive. While the findings of Banks, Cresswell and Ainley found no relationship between test results and computer availability,[3] a study conducted by Wenglinsky on American students a few years earlier found that access to computers in the home had an adverse impact on pupils' achievement.[4] Wenglinsky's findings were supported by Fuchs and Woessmann in their major study involving data from over 30 countries.[5] Conversely, Harrison et al. in their research within the United Kingdom found that computers and technology had a positive impact on learning.[6]

While the studies outlined above demonstrate the divergence of opinions on the value of technology in education, it is important to acknowledge that neither technology nor education is a monolithic entity with uniform functions or aims. It seems self-evident that a computer could be either a help or a hindrance to learning, depending on how it is used. Moreover, the aims of education are typically more varied than test scores which are easily subject to quantitative analysis. This is certainly true of many involved within Holocaust education. Studies like those of Wenglinsky which focus on student achievement in Mathematics seem to be measuring something quite removed from what a teacher of history or citizenship for example might be trying to achieve.

Like with so many other aspects of Holocaust education, the value and importance of new technologies can only be assessed when the aims and purposes of teaching the subject have first been established. If practitioners are primarily aiming to educate students on the history of the Holocaust, then the impact of new technology is perhaps easier to gauge than broader ambitions which may want to influence moral outlooks.

DOI: 10.1057/9781137388575.0010

Despite the differences of opinion regarding both the pedagogic value of technology and the aims of Holocaust education, it is indubitable that in recent years there has been something of a digital revolution across the globe which has had important consequences for the field. While the impact of this on teaching and learning generally has naturally varied, it has also affected the nature of Holocaust education, generating various challenges and opportunities. Moreover, it raises many valuable questions with which the field will increasingly need to grapple and seek to answer. These include, but are by no means limited to questions such as, how are students using existing technologies such as social media in relation to their knowledge and understanding of the Holocaust? How can technology help to tackle some of the problems which the field faces, both now and in the future? What direction is Holocaust pedagogy likely to take in an increasingly digital era of education?

Giving survivors a voice

Emerging technologies have helped to provide solutions to a number of the challenges which the field of Holocaust education faces. As discussed in Chapter 5, some of the greatest concerns are connected to teaching the subject in a post-survivor era and how to make the best use of the archival material which has been recorded. One of these dilemmas is the dissemination of such an abundance of testimony material. With the quantity of Holocaust survivor testimonies totalling hundreds of thousands of hours, it seems very difficult to find the exact material which is needed or to ensure that every voice is heard.

Within the Museum of the Holocaust in Los Angeles, a 'tree of testimony' has been designed whereby, according to Rothman, 'sixty-five screens, seemingly placed at random across a large wall, are connected via wires that suggest the branches of a "tree of life," or family tree.'[7] The testimonies which are played on the screens, collectively form 105,000 hours of video from over 50,000 survivors but mean that each account will be played at least once a year. Through the use of an iPod touch-based audio-guidance system and a sophisticated search engine with over 50,000 search items, museum visitors can find specific extracts of individual testimonies which relate to the area in which they are interested.[8] This means that testimonies are not simply an archival witness to the experiences of the past, but a usable database which is easily accessed by the public as well as the scholar.

DOI: 10.1057/9781137388575.0010

This is an area in which further work is needed. The vast amounts of material mean that common themes which appear in the testimonies need to be connected. If one survivor for example is talking about a specific experience or a particular village, it seems helpful for the listener to be able to follow this up with similar or connecting accounts. Hintze has highlighted two models he has developed in advancing this particular area, 'one for clustering testimonies with a common theme, and another for examining the relationships between keywords to make it easier to find testimonies with common narratives'.[9] It seems that if the use of survivor testimonies is going to have a significant impact on classroom teaching, then it needs to be made user-friendly for both teachers and students alike, so that they can search and select the appropriate testimonies quickly and easily. Moreover, time constraints seldom allow for lengthy accounts to be played in full. Dividing testimonies into specific sections to match search terms may also enhance their use within the field of education.

Hajič, Ircing and Psutka highlight two important limitations which exist on searching testimony archives. The first of these is that someone may wish to search for a word which is not indexed as a keyword, while the other is the problem of testimonies which are not in the language of the person conducting the search. Project 'AMALACH', which is being carried out with the support of the Czech Republic's Ministry of Culture, is seeking to tackle these problems by using a speech-recognition engine, which 'after being presented with thousands of recorded vocal utterances and corresponding text transcriptions ... develops a statistical framework for assessing the likelihood that a specific unit of sound relates to a specific unit of text'.[10] In addition to this, software is being developed to ensure that words which are searched for in one's native language can generate results from testimonies in a number of different languages.

Furthermore, new developments in technology have recently evolved so that relevant and precise survivor testimonies no longer need to be searched for by the user but can be automatically generated by their specific geographical location. This is achieved through the use of Broadcastr, a smartphone app available for the iPhone and Android. Through collaboration between the application provider and the USC Visual History Archive, people can view testimony which is directly connected to the location which they are visiting. As Lindenbaum states, 'for example, if someone with the Broadcastr app visited Auschwitz-Birkenau, testimony of those who had survived the camp could start playing automatically

DOI: 10.1057/9781137388575.0010

based on the visitor's location.'" This innovative idea could revolutionise the way that school visits to Holocaust-related sites integrate testimony into their experiences.

The ability to search Holocaust testimonies has been an important part of IWitness, the online educational programme of the USC Shoah Foundation's testimony programme. The website was recognised as one of the 'Best Websites for Teaching and Learning' by the American Association of School Librarians in 2012, and has been accessed by around 6,000 students and 2,000 educators in 35 countries.[12] One of the key features of the website has been the IWitness Video Challenge which enables students to design and construct their own projects using the built-in online video editing facilities. This highlights an area where cross-curricular collaboration can occur as students develop their historical knowledge and acquire or develop new skills in technology.

According to a study by Cole, Street and Felt, which was conducted on 136 high school students and 75 educators, the impact of the IWitness programme was both profound and positive. They remarked that educators 'reported the observable and measurable impact of IWitness' digital testimonies on learners',[13] such as an increase in students' willingness to speak out against stereotyping and racism. In contrast to the assessments of many other curriculums and initiatives, 'plans are underway for more longitudinal studies on the cognitive and affective impact of watching and editing video testimony – an important form of digital storytelling – on IWitness users'.[14]

Social media

The use of smartphone devices has been instrumental in the success of social media and at the forefront of this digital revolution has been the microblogging site Twitter, which enables users to follow individuals and organisations and to directly communicate with them. By using a hash tag, it also means that trends can be followed which relate to certain themes or terms. In relation to Holocaust education, it seems that Twitter has a lot of potential for helping students develop their academic interests outside of school and keep up with the latest information and developments. Various Holocaust organisations such as the USHMM, which to date have over 165,000 followers (October 2013), regularly tweet significant anniversaries, links to survivor stories, training opportunities

DOI: 10.1057/9781137388575.0010

or details of forthcoming events. The interactive nature of Twitter is already being harnessed to develop educational initiatives. Organisations like the USHMM, for example, provide occasions when individuals can tweet them questions about a specific topic such as 'Responsibility to Protect' which they will then answer. This enables students from all over the world to ask questions which can receive an answer from global experts. On other occasions, individuals have the opportunity to tweet questions to a survivor whose answers are tweeted back on the site's feed. Twitter also allows for live tweeting whereby speeches or events can be reported around the world in real time. On 22 March 2013, for example, Yad Vashem (as well as various media organisations) live tweeted the visit of Barack Obama. Opportunities to utilise Twitter within the field of Holocaust education already abound both inside and outside the classroom, although it seems probable that many teachers would like training on how to maximise its potential within a pedagogic setting.

Despite the potential value of social media in Holocaust education, there are also concerns which have been raised. In her groundbreaking paper, 'The Holocaust and Social Networks: Memory, Commemoration or Forums for Anti-Semitism and Racism?',[15] Pfanzelter suggests that the social media is also being used to spread right wing extremism and Holocaust denial. The blogosphere in this area has been particularly active in the last few years, in contrast to traditional Holocaust-related blogs. Right wing and anti-Semitic organisations tend to express their ideas outside of mainstream social networking sites like Facebook due to the regulations which govern their use. Nevertheless, in his detailed study of Holocaust denial in the USA, Darnell found 31 Facebook groups which have 'the denial of the Holocaust as their central or predominant purpose' collectively consisting of 4,853 members.[16]

As Pfanzelter recognises, Facebook has also been used as a medium for Holocaust memorialisation. Examples of this include the setting up of Facebook pages for Holocaust victims such as Henio Zytomirski, who was murdered in Majdanek in 1942 and with whom Facebook users until 2010 could become 'friends'. Pages also exist for Anne Frank, with user comments showing that many people post on the page as though they were speaking to Anne Frank directly with some individuals indicating that they believed her to consequently still be alive. Clearly, such Facebook pages offer problems and opportunities. They raise ethical issues about the morality of speaking on behalf of the deceased in the first person, yet they raise awareness of the tragedies which befell the

DOI: 10.1057/9781137388575.0010

victims, preserve their memories and may educate individuals about their experiences. Nevertheless, scholars such as Murray have argued that digital technology and especially the use of pictures is now 'more about an immediate, rather fleeting, display and collection of one's discovery and framing of the small and mundane'.[17] If this is the case, which seems very plausible, then Facebook pages such as these may only be contributing to the trivialisation of the Holocaust.

Even stronger claims of Holocaust trivialisation might be made against the way that the subject is sometimes used through the medium of YouTube videos. This is certainly the argument which is powerfully put forward in Hansen's interestingly named paper, 'Auschwitz is made of Lego and Hitler hates Beckham: YouTube and the Future of Holocaust Remembrance'.[18] He argues that parodies of the scene from the film *Downfall* showing Hitler's extreme anger have become incredibly popular and that users' comments show flippancy and humour, suggesting that for many young people the Holocaust is no longer reverent nor the time period perceived to be relevant. Hansen highlights the fact that Hitler being banned from the X-Box has over 8 million views to date, while the video of Hitler intending to murder Justin Bieber led to some users posting comments such as 'Hitler is my hero now'. Hansen's empirical research led him to argue that the makers of Nazi or Holocaust-related videos, such as Lego motion (using Lego animation), have conducted no historical research before making and uploading their productions.

The studies of Pfanzelter and Hansen are incredibly valuable contributions to the field of Holocaust studies and have particular resonance in the field of education. According to a 2010 study by the Kaiser Family Foundation, young people in America between the age of 8 and 18 spend over seven hours a day consuming media,[19] while a study of online habits among UK adolescents suggested that they spend 31 hours a week online with around two hours a week on YouTube and chat rooms.[20] To date, there is a distinct absence of research on how the internet and in particular social media impact on students' knowledge and understanding of the Holocaust, as well as the way that they perceive the subject in terms of its relevance and importance.

It also seems apparent that greater work needs to be done to ensure that social media can be used positively and effectively in Holocaust education. Only by a closer analysis of young people's online habits, patterns and tastes can education realise the potential of the digital age.

DOI: 10.1057/9781137388575.0010

Adolescents today have access to more information than ever before, yet this means that there is also greater availability of inaccurate or prejudicial material which will undermine the efforts of those engaged in teaching the Holocaust. This is highlighted by Darnell's valuable study where he found that one of the largest Holocaust denial websites was receiving on average over 200,000 unique visitors each month during 2009. He also found that by using search engines to ask many legitimate questions such as 'When did the Holocaust start?' could lead to denial-related websites. Darnell correctly asserts:

> Holocaust denial on the Internet becomes an especially concerning problem when well-meaning people (possibly students or curious adults) search for the answers to straightforward, factual questions about the Holocaust and end up finding websites devoted to Holocaust denial.[21]

In their article 'White Supremacists, Oppositional Culture and the World Wide Web', Adams and Roscigno highlight that Neo-Nazi groups often associate themselves with issues such as Holocaust denial and that 'the internet is a dominant new technology that is inexpensive and easily accessible, proving to be a valuable resource to social movement organizations striving to disseminate information and attract new members'.[22]

In addition to more work being needed in this area, scholars in the field of Holocaust education have largely ignored (with some exceptions like Pfanzelter) using Google trends, which show the patterns which have occurred in users' searches. This resource also provides graphical data for the trends in YouTube searches as well. Although it is impossible to know whether or not it is students who are making these searches, general trends cannot be ignored and are likely to reflect patterns which are replicated among adolescents as well. One of the rare uses of Google trends in scholarship in Holocaust education is found in Darnell's work. He noted:

> While the relative popularity of searches of the term 'Holocaust' has trended downwards since 2004, the relative popularity of searches of 'Holocaust denial' is on the rise. Specifically, over the past year, the use of 'denial' as a related search term to the Holocaust has increased by seventy per cent.[23]

Since the publication of Darnell's findings in 2010, the downward trend in searching for the term 'Holocaust' has continued and highlights the need to garner the internet's ever-evolving potential to engage and educate learners in effective and absorbing ways.

DOI: 10.1057/9781137388575.0010

One such example of this is the establishing of a YouTube channel, showing over 100 full-length survivor testimonies as well as various scholarly lectures, which has been established by the USC Shoah Foundation Institute for Visual History and Education. Moreover, through Visual History Archive on the Internet (VHA-I) 1,000 English-language testimonies will be uploaded so that 'students will be able to work with testimony and other resources, individually or cooperatively, in an online environment moderated by their teachers'.[24]

The ubiquity of social media in many adolescents' lives clearly provides opportunities and challenges. Fanning argues that children know how to use Facebook and Twitter but struggle to adapt their technological abilities to a learning environment and to use this technology for educational purposes like the study of the Holocaust.[25] Perhaps this highlights a pedagogic problem which transcends Holocaust education specifically.

Web-based learning

In addition to social media, various web-based learning already exists within the field of Holocaust education, with other pioneering developments currently being worked on. Jaeger correctly states that 'it is not surprising to find that there is a great deal of Holocaust coverage on the Internet. Yet there is a kind of unevenness to the Holocaust sites, with some focused on personal and individual experiences and others of broader scope'.[26] Despite this, Cassutto advocates teaching the Holocaust with the internet by suggesting that 'students have a medium of self-expression and cultural exchange' as well as an 'interactive medium' where 'the user decides what to do and where to go'.[27] These so-called advantages could be a cause of concern, especially in light of Darnell's findings on the extent of Holocaust denial which exists on the internet.

Nevertheless, online Holocaust education is not a homogenous form of pedagogy with Fanning drawing a distinction between 'shallow learning', where information is simply provided, and deeper learning, which involves interaction, understanding and engagement.[28] In an attempt to achieve the latter, Fanning established a virtual learning environment to both discuss the Holocaust and other genocides and to prepare students for the visit of a survivor. In addition to this Fanning sought to 'test the hypothesis that social media applications could support school based Holocaust education'.[29] Interestingly, he concluded that this project was

DOI: 10.1057/9781137388575.0010

by no means as successful as he might have hoped and that there were practical limitations, with students failing to engage as effectively as was necessary.[30]

Conversely, Lazar and Hirsch found that question-and-answer online communities were immensely popular for discussing the Holocaust.[31] In their empirical study of the 'Yahoo! Answers' community, they analysed responses to those who needed help with their homework, such as questions to ask a Holocaust survivor or the writing of an essay on Holocaust remembrance. Lazar and Hirsch found that answers were 'in most cases based upon their own views and reflect common notions, and are rarely accepted by askers'. They concluded by suggesting that scholars and educators involved in Holocaust remembrance education ought to develop a closer relationship with the medium as children's ideas and understandings may well be informed by such online communities to a considerable extent.

One of the boldest and most innovative web-based projects, which is currently being developed by Conscience Design and the USC Institute for Creative Technologies, is 'New Dimensions in Testimony'. Using over 6,000 LED lights and a 26-foot spherical stage, survivors' responses are filmed to produce a three dimensional hologram-like digital projection which can be used to interact with the students of the future. Answers are recorded which directly respond to the typical questions which students ask, enabling future generations to feel as though they are actually engaging and interacting with the survivors. The technology provides a depth to the hologram, which is truly three dimensional and even allows the representation to make realistic eye contact. Alongside this is a programme called Natural Language Understanding which generates the most appropriate answer to the question that is posed from the bank of answers which will be recorded in this fashion. According to Maio, Traum and Debevec, the aim of the project is to create 'an environment in which an individual or an entire class can have a survivor sit with them to tell his or her story, via video or projector; they will be able to ask questions, and the survivor will answer from the testimony as if he or she were in the room'.[32]

The 'New Dimensions in Testimony' project seems to go a step further than the existing work which has been carried out in the field of survivor testimonies. Rather than simply seeking to preserve the accounts and stories of those who experienced the Holocaust, it attempts to give the impression that the survivor themselves are still alive and that their

DOI: 10.1057/9781137388575.0010

insights and wisdom can be passed on in person to every successive generation. The project works on the belief that it is more than the testimonies themselves which are important within pedagogy. In addition to their experiences is the connection and bond which can emerge between the survivor and the student. Majo, Traum and Debevec express this when they write:

> Countless children have been touched by Holocaust survivors who have visited their school or talked to them in a museum. These encounters have created a connection and given those students an intimate experience with someone uniquely qualified to reflect on life, and about a very real part of history from an eyewitness perspective.[33]

While the experiences of students using the 'New Dimensions in Testimony' project are likely to be more personal and engaging than watching a video, which does not directly respond to their questions, it seems unlikely that students will feel the same connection which they do when they meet a survivor in the flesh and can ask personal questions and enter into real dialogue, rather than mere questioning. Consequently it seems that though the most advanced digital technology can assist in developing Holocaust education, there are limitations to it. It will never be able to replicate with the same emotional depth the experiences which are presently available to those students who spend time with survivors.

While the 'New Dimensions in Testimony' generate three dimensional holograms of survivors, pioneering technology, which is being applied to Holocaust education, is attempting to develop a fourth dimension. The Integrated Media Systems Center at the University of Southern California creates computer-generated 'virtual spaces' which show how something has changed over time in a concept known as geo-immersion. According to Shahabi, Khodaei and Fishbain:

> 4-D 'virtual spaces' are 3-D buildings and places built up from original maps and plans, which change with time, making a fourth dimension. It means that if you view the space as it was in 1940, it will be different from 1944 and very different from the current day.[34]

This technology offers a number of opportunities within the field of Holocaust education. It would provide a very useful resource for students to see the changes that occurred on a street, in a ghetto or in a concentration camp. If this technology became available on portable devices, such as through a smartphone application, one might also be

DOI: 10.1057/9781137388575.0010

able to integrate it into their experiences of visiting historical sites, in a similar way to the Broadcastr application discussed earlier in the chapter. Geo-Immersion may one day be successfully integrated with survivor testimonies, although to do so involves technical challenges such as using 'text, space and time features to "rank" the testimonies so that searches yield the most relevant results'.[35] Yet such integrated and ambitious targets are the goal of those involved with this technology as Shahabi, Khodaei and Fishbain explain:

> Using geo-immersion, we aim to place the testimonies of Holocaust survivors within a 4-D space, such as an interface that would allow a student or researcher to 'walk' through a simulated location – a historical site, for instance – observing how it looked 70 years ago compared to how it looks today, all while listening to relevant testimony about the location and the events that occurred there.[36]

If such a project was to come to fruition, it might revolutionise the nature of Holocaust education especially outside of the classroom when visiting historical sites. It would offer an unprecedented insight into the past with the potential to integrate the voice of survivors into the exploration of the place which is being discovered.

The future of Holocaust education

It is difficult to say with any confidence the technological direction of the future and perhaps most importantly, the ways in which that will affect Holocaust education. Nevertheless the high speed of change certainly seems likely to continue. In the light of this it is imperative that sufficient training is available for practitioners so that they can become confident and savvy in their use of the technology. Yet the training that occurs needs to go beyond simply showing how the programmes and software work, but how they can be best employed to fulfil the specific goals of Holocaust education. According to a 2006 report by JESNA, 'teachers [in the US] are uncomfortable using technology and are unaware of all it offers, both to increase their own historical knowledge and to create learning activities for students.'[37] This is something which is beginning to be challenged, with the USC Shoah Foundation, for example, providing specialist training in teaching with testimony, which to date has been implemented in Ukraine, the Czech Republic, Hungary and Poland among others.[38]

DOI: 10.1057/9781137388575.0010

It many cases, it may be a long time before some of the technology discussed in this chapter is commonly used. Some of the projects may fall along the wayside, either through lack of funding or a rejection of their pedagogic value. This highlights an important caution. In the same way that Holocaust education has consistently returned to the question of aims and purposes, so do these issues need to lie at the heart of technological advances in the field. Often the scientific developments are being led by specialists in technology and not by those who are sensitive to the historical and pedagogic issues which are so complicated and central to Holocaust education. The direction and practical application of the technology therefore needs to be determined by those who understand the questions and debates which exist within the field. This is likely to lead to greater collaboration between specialists in Holocaust education and those who are developing and pioneering the technology. This important relationship is likely to benefit both parties.

In addition to training practitioners in how to best utilise the technology in their teaching, pupils too need careful guidance. Despite many young people possessing advanced digital skills, students often struggle to understand the educational potential of various technologies and how to apply their existing understanding to further their learning.

The nature of the developments which are explained in this chapter also suggests that the character of teaching and the means of interactions will increasingly transcend traditional learning environments and the boundaries of the classroom. Much of the technology allows for students to discover things for themselves through portable devices and web-based learning. This highlights the importance of educating adolescents on how to best maximise their learning through these more autonomous means.

Holocaust education is an ever-evolving field and has developed significantly over the last decade as this book demonstrates. The pace of change for the next ten years seems unlikely to slow down. While few things are certain with regards to the direction that is taken, it seems that Holocaust survivor Branko Lustig is correct when he states:

> The next generation will tell their own story in their own words with whatever means they have at their disposal. Our job is not to dissuade them from using their voice and the technology at their fingertips but rather to encourage them to do it with care, with dignity, and humanity.[39]

DOI: 10.1057/9781137388575.0010

Notes

1   Hew, K. F. and Brush, T. (2007) 'Integrating Technology into K–12 Teaching and Learning: Current Knowledge Gaps and Recommendations for Future Research', *Educational Technology Research and Development*, 55: 3, 223–252, p. 224.
2   Daniel, J. (2007) 'The Economist Debate Series. Proposition: The Continuing Introduction of New Technologies and New Media Adds Little to the Quality of Most Education'. Available: http://www.economist.com/.
3   Banks, D., Cresswell, J. and Ainley, J. (2003) 'Higher Order Learning and ICT Amongst Australian 15 Year Olds'. Paper presented at the International Congress of School Effectiveness and Improvement, Sydney.
4   Wenglinsky, H. (1998) *Does It Compute? The Relationship between Educational Technology and Student Achievement in Mathematics,* (Princeton, NJ: Policy Information Center of the Educational Testing Service).
5   Fuchs, T. and Woessmann, L. (2004) 'Computers and Student Learning: Bivariate and Multivariate Evidence on the Availability and Use of Computers at Home and at School', CESifo Working Paper Series 1321, CESifo Group Munich.
6   Harrison, C., Comber, C., Fisher, T., Haw, K., Lunzer, E., McFarlane, A., Mavers, D., Scrimshaw, P., Somekh, B. and Watling, R. (2002) *ImpaCT2: The Impact of Information and Communication Technologies on Pupil Learning and Attainment,* (Coventry: Becta).
7   Rothman, M. (2010) 'Building a Tree of Testimony', *Past Forward*, Summer 2010, 17, p. 17.
8   Rothman, 'Building a Tree', p. 17.
9   Hintze, M. (2012) 'A Surprising Quantum', *Past Forward*, Summer 2012, 12–13, p. 13.
10 Hajič, J., Ircing, P. and Psutka, J. (2012) 'Searching Their Voices', *Past Forward*, Summer 2012, 28–29, p. 28.
11 Lindenbaum, S. (2012) 'Testimony on Location', *Past Forward*, Summer 2012, 10–11, pp.10–11.
12 USC Shoah Foundation. Available: http://sfi.usc.edu/about Accessed 1 October 2013.
13 Cole, G., Street, K. and Felt, L. (2013) 'Storytelling in the Digital Age: Engaging Learners for Cognitive and Affective Gains', *The International Journal of Technology, Knowledge and Society*, 8: 6, 113–119, p. 116.
14 Cole, Street and Felt, 'Storytelling in the Digital Age', p. 117.
15 Pfanzelter, E. (2013) 'The Holocaust and Social Networks: Memory, Commemoration or Forums for Anti-Semitism and Racism?' Paper presented at *The Future of Holocaust Studies Conference*, Universities of Southampton and Winchester, 29–31 July 2013.

DOI: 10.1057/9781137388575.0010

16   Darnell, S. (2010) *Measuring Holocaust Denial in the United States*, (Policy Analysis Exercise, MA: Harvard Kennedy School of Government), p. 33.

17   Murray, S. (2008) 'Digital Images, Photo-Sharing, and Our Shifting Notions of Everyday Aesthetics', *Journal of Visual Culture*, 7: 2, 147–163, p. 147.

18   Hansen, J. (2013) 'Auschwitz Is Made of Lego and Hitler Hates Beckham: YouTube and the Future of Holocaust Remembrance'. Paper presented at *The Future of Holocaust Studies Conference*, Universities of Southampton and Winchester, 29–31 July 2013.

19   Rideout, V., Foehr, U. and Roberts, D. (2010) *Generation M2: Media in the Lives of 8- to 18-Year Olds*, (California: A Kaiser Family Foundation Study).

20   'Teenagers "spend an average of 31 hours online"'. http://www.telegraph.co.uk Accessed 3 October 2013.

21   Darnell, *Measuring Holocaust Denial*, p. 38.

22   Adams, J. and Roscigno, V. (2005) 'White Supremacists, Oppositional Culture and the World Wide Web', *Social Forces*, 84: 2, 759–778, p. 775.

23   Darnell, *Measuring Holocaust Denial*, p. 33.

24   Smith, S. (2010) 'Online: First Testimonies on the Internet', *Past Forward*, Summer 2010, p. 3.

25   Fanning, J. (2013) 'Going Online: Supporting Classroom Teaching and Learning about the Holocaust'. Paper presented at *The Future of Holocaust Studies Conference*, Universities of Southampton and Winchester, 29–31 July 2013.

26   Jaeger, J. (2010) 'Holocaust Resources on the Web', *College and Research Libraries News*, 71: 2, 80–87.

27   Cassutto, G. (2004) 'Teaching the Holocaust with the Internet'. Paper presented at *Teaching the Holocaust to Future Generations* Conference, Yad Vashem, Jerusalem, 1–10, p. 1.

28   Fanning, 'Going Online'.

29   Fanning, J. (2013) 'It's Good to Talk: Supporting Holocaust Education through Online Conferencing', Unpublished Report for the Centre for Holocaust Education, Institute of Education, University of London.

30   Fanning, 'Going Online'.

31   Lazar, A. and Hirsch, T. (2013) 'An Online Partner for Holocaust Remembrance Education: Students Approaching the Yahoo! Answers Community', *Educational Review*, DOI: 10.1080/00131911.2013.839545.

32   Maio, H., Traum, D. and Debevec, P. (2012) 'New Dimensions in Testimony', *Past Forward*, Summer 2012, 22–26, p. 24.

33   Maio et al., 'New Dimensions in Testimony', p. 24.

34   Shahabi, C., Khodaei, A. and Fishbain, B. (2012) 'Geo-Immersive Learning', *Past Forward*, Summer 2012, 11–12, p. 11.

35   Shahabi et al., 'Geo-Immersive Learning', p. 12.

36   Shahabi et al., 'Geo-Immersive Learning', p. 11.

DOI: 10.1057/9781137388575.0010

37   Isaacs, L., Rosov, W., Raff, L., Rosenblatt, S., Hecht, S., Rozenek, M. and
     Rotem, Z. (2006) 'Best Practices in Holocaust Education': Report to the San
     Francisco Jewish Community Endowment Fund, Jewish Education Service
     of North America, p. 16.
38   USC Shoah Foundation. Available: http://sfi.usc.edu/about Accessed 1
     October 2013.
39   Lustig, B. (2013) 'When Everything Changed', *Past Forward*, Summer 2012,
     6–9, p. 6.

DOI: 10.1057/9781137388575.0010

Bibliography

Adams, J. and Roscigno, V. (2005) 'White Supremacists, Oppositional Culture and the World Wide Web', *Social Forces*, 84: 2, 759–778.

Alexander, J. C. (2002) 'On the Social Construction of Moral Universals: The 'Holocaust' from War Crime to Trauma Drama', *European Journal of Social Theory*, 5: 1, 5–85.

Andrews, K. (2013) 'A Damned Good Cry', *Past Forward*, Summer 2013, 14–15.

Andrews, K., Gray, M. and Maws, A. (2013) 'Responses to BJ Epstein's "Inflicting Trauma"', *Holocaust Studies: A Journal of Culture and History*, 19: 1, 121–134.

Auron, Y. (2003) *The Pain of Knowledge: Holocaust and Genocide Issues in Education* (London: Transaction Publishers).

Avraham, D. (2010) 'The Problem with using Historical Parallels as a Method in Holocaust and Genocide Teaching', *Intercultural Education*, 21: S1, S33–S40.

Balberg, E. (1999) *The Impact of the Holocaust Literature and Film.* Paper presented at Yad Vashem, 14 October 1999.

Banks, D., Cresswell, J. and Ainley, J. (2003) 'Higher Order Learning and ICT amongst Australian 15 Year Olds'. Paper presented at the International Congress of School Effectiveness and Improvement, Sydney.

Bardige, B. (1983) *Reflective Thinking and Prosocial Awareness: Adolescents Face the Holocaust and Themselves.* Unpublished Dissertation (Harvard University).

Barnouw, D. (1998) *Anne Frank: voor Beginners en Gevorderden* (Den Haag: Sdu).

Barr, D. (2005) 'Early Adolescents' Reflections on Social Justice: Facing History and Ourselves in Practice and Assessment', *Intercultural Education*, 16: 2, 145–160.

Bartov, O. (2011) 'Setting the Record Straight', *Past Forward*, Spring 2011, 24–26.

Bastel, H., Mtzka, C. and Miklas, H. (2010) 'Holocaust Education in Austria: A (Hi)story of Complexity and Ambivalence', *Prospects*, 40: 1, 57–73.

Bauer, Y. (1994) 'Conclusion: The Significance of the Final Solution', in Cesarani, D. (Ed.) *The Final Solution: Origins and Implementation* (London: Routledge).

Bauer, Y. (2001) *Re-thinking the Holocaust* (New Haven: Yale University Press).

Beaver, C. (2013) 'IWitness Evaluation Report', *Past Forward*, Summer 2013, 30–32.

Berenbaum, M. and Kramer, A. (1993) *The World Must Know: The History of the Holocaust as Told in the United States Holocaust Memorial Museum* (Washington DC: USHMM).

Bhana, K. (2012) 'Case Study 5: Is Teaching about the Holocaust Suitable for Primary Aged Children?' *Primary History*, Summer, 29 30.

Bialystok, F. (1996) 'Americanizing the Holocaust: Beyond the Limit of the Universal', in Millen, R. L. (Ed.) *New Perspectives on the Holocaust* (New York and London: New York University Press).

Bischoping, K. (1998) 'Method and Meaning in Holocaust-Knowledge Surveys', *Holocaust and Genocide Studies*, 12: 3, 454–474.

Block, B. (2013) 'Blog'. www.rabbiblock.com.

Błuszkowski, J. (2005) *Stereotypy a to Zsamos´c´ Narodowa* [Stereotypes and National Identity]. (Warsaw: Dom Wydawniczy Elipsa).

Blutinger, J. (2009) 'Bearing Witness: Teaching the Holocaust from a Victim-Centred Perspective', *The History Teacher*, 42: 3, 269–279.

BBC (2013) 'Pope Likens Abortions to Holocaust'. www.bbc.co.uk.

Browning, C. (2003) *Collected Memories: Holocaust History and Postwar Testimony* (London: University of Wisconsin Press).

Browning, C. (2011) 'Remembering Survival', *Past Forward*, Spring 2011, 18–19.

Byford, J. (2010) ' "Shortly Afterwards, We Heard the Sound of the Gas Van": Survivor Testimony and the Writing of History in Socialist Yugolslavia', *History and Memory*, 22: 1, 5–47.

DOI: 10.1057/9781137388575.0011

Caldwell, J. (2011) *Holocaust Consciousness in New Zealand 1980–2010: A Study*. Unpublished MA Thesis (Victoria University, Wellington).

Carr, H. (2012) *How Do Children in an Egyptian International School Respond to the Teaching of the Holocaust?* Unpublished MEd thesis (University of Hull).

Cassutto, G. (2004) 'Teaching the Holocaust with the Internet'. Paper presented at *Teaching the Holocaust to Future Generations* Conference (Yad Vashem, Jerusalem), 1–10.

Chyrikins, M. and Vieyra, M. (2010) 'Making the Past Relevant to Future Generations: The Work of the Anne Frank House in Latin America', *Intercultural Education*, 21: S1, S7–S15.

Clark, M. M. (2005) 'Holocaust Video Testimony, Oral History and Narrative Medicine: The Struggle against Indifference', *Literature and Medicine*, 24: 2, 266–282.

Clements, J. (2006) 'A Very Neutral Voice: Teaching about the Holocaust', *Educate*, 5: 1, 39–49.

Clyde, C. (2010) 'Developing Civic Leaders through an Experiential Learning Programme for Holocaust Education', *Prospects*, 40: 2, 289–306.

Cohen, E. (2008) *Youth Tourism to Israel: Educational Experiences of the Diaspora* (Clevedon UK: Channel View Publications).

Cohen, E. (2009) *Echoes and Reflections 2008–2009*. Yad Vashem and ADL. Unpublished Report.

Cohen, E. (2013) *Identity and Pedagogy: Shoah Education in Israeli State Schools* (Brighton, MA: Academic Studies Press).

Cohen-Almagor, R. (2008) 'Hate in the Classroom: Free Expression, Holocaust Denial, and Liberal Education', *American Journal of Education*, 114, 215–241.

Cole, T. (2000) *Selling the Holocaust* (New York: Routledge).

Cole, G., Street, K. and Felt, L. (2013) 'Storytelling in the Digital Age: Engaging Learners for Cognitive and Affective Gains', *The International Journal of Technology, Knowledge and Society*, 8: 6, 113–119.

Cowan, P. and Maitles, H. (2007) 'Does Addressing Prejudice and Discrimination through Holocaust Education Produce Better Citizens?' *Educational Review*, 59: 2, 115–130.

Cowan, P. and Maitles, H. (2011) ' "We Saw Inhumanity Close Up". What Is Gained by School Students from Scotland Visiting Auschwitz?', *Journal of Curriculum Studies*, 43: 2, 163–184.

DOI: 10.1057/9781137388575.0011

Daniel, J. (2007) The Economist Debate Series. Proposition: The
    Continuing Introduction of New Technologies and New Media
    Adds Little to the Quality of Most Education. Available: http://www.
    economist.com/
Darnell, S. (2010) *Measuring Holocaust Denial in the United States*, Policy
    Analysis Exercise (MA: Harvard Kennedy School of Government).
Davis, B. and Rubinstein-Avila, E. (2013) 'Holocaust Education:
    Global Forces Shaping Curricula Integration and Implementation',
    Intercultural Education, 24: 1–2, 149–166.
De Vaus, D. (2007) *Surveys in Social Research*, 5th ed. (London:
    Routledge).
Doneson, J. (2002) 'Introduction', in Doneson, J. (Ed.) *The Holocaust in
    American Film* (New York: Syracuse University Press) 1–12.
Donovan, M. S. and Bransford, J. D. (2005) 'Introduction', in Donovan,
    M. S. and Bransford, J. D. (Eds) *How Students Learn. History in the
    Classroom* (Washington DC: National Academies Press) 1–28.
Dreier, W., Herscovitch, A. and Polak, K. (2013) 'A Slowly Escaping
    Landscape', *Past Forward*, Summer 2013, 32–34.
Eckmann, M. (2010) 'Exploring the Relevance of Holocaust Education
    for Human Rights Education', *Prospects*, 40: 17–16.
Economist (2013) 'Bearing Witness Evermore'. www.economist.com.
    Accessed 3 September 2013.
Edwards, C. and O'Dowd, S. (2010) 'The Edge of Knowing: Investigating
    Students' Prior Understandings of the Holocaust', *Teaching History*,
    141, 20–26.
Ene, C. (2013) 'Teaching the Holocaust with the Use of Active
    Learning Methods: The Case of a Lower Secondary School with
    a High Number of Neo-Nazi Supporters in Northern Greece', in
    *ICERI2013 Proceedings: 6ᵗʰ International Conference of Education,
    Research and Innovation*, Seville, Spain, 18–20 November 2013,
    3758–3764.
Epstein, B. J. (2013) 'Inflicting Trauma: The Ethics of Writing and
    Teaching the Holocaust for Children', *Holocaust Studies: A Journal of
    Culture and History*, 19: 1, 101–120.
Facing History and Ourselves (2013) www.facinghistory.org
Fallace, T. (2008) *The Emergence of Holocaust Education in American
    Schools* (New York: Palgrave Macmillan).
Fanning, J. (2013) 'Going Online: Supporting Classroom Teaching
    and Learning about the Holocaust'. Paper presented at *The Future*

of Holocaust Studies Conference, Universities of Southampton and Winchester, 29–31 July 2013.

Fanning, J. (2013) 'It's Good to Talk: Supporting Holocaust Education through Online Conferencing', Unpublished Report for the Centre for Holocaust Education, Institute of Education, University of London.

Flanz, H. (Ed.) (1999) *The Americanization of the Holocaust* (Maryland: The John Hopkins University Press).

Foster, S. (2013) 'Teaching about the Holocaust in English Schools: Challenges and Possibilities', *Intercultural Education*, 24: 1–2, 133–148.

Frank, M. (2013) 'The Holocaust Taken in Vain to Promote Gun Rights'. www.theguardian.com

Frankl, M. (2003) 'Holocaust Education in the Czech Republic, 1989–2002', *Intercultural Education*, 14: 2, 177–189.

Friedländer, H. (1980) 'Towards a Methodology of Teaching about the Holocaust', in Friedlander, H. and Milton, S. (Eds) *The Holocaust: Ideology, Bureaucracy and Genocide*, The San Jose Papers, The National Conference of Christians and Jews, 1980.

Friedländer, S. (2007) *Nazi Germany and the Jews 1939–45: The Years of Extermination* (New York: HarperCollins).

Fuchs, T. and Woessmann, L. (2004) 'Computers and Student Learning: Bivariate and Multivariate Evidence on the Availability and Use of Computers at Home and at School', CESifo Working Paper Series 1321, CESifo Group Munich.

Gerstenfeld, M. (2009) *The Abuse of Holocaust Memory: Distortions and Responses* (Jerusalem: Jerusalem Center for Public Affairs).

Glanz, J. (1999) 'Ten Suggestions for Teaching the Holocaust', *The History Teacher*, 32: 4, 547–565.

Gold, T., Kennedy, R., Levi, T. and Reiss, F. (2005) 'The Survivors Right to Reply', in Haggith, T. and Newman, J. (Eds) *Holocaust and the Moving Image: Representations in Film and Television since 1933* (London: Wallflower Press).

Golub, J. and Cohen, R. (1993) *What Do Americans Know about the Holocaust?* (New York: American Jewish Committee).

Gray, M. (2011) 'Understanding Pupil Preconceptions of the Holocaust in English Schools', *Holocaust Studies: A Journal of Culture and History*, 17: 1, 1–28.

Gray, M. (2013) 'The Boy in the Striped Pyjamas: A Blessing or Curse for Holocaust Educators?' Paper presented at *The Future of Holocaust*

DOI: 10.1057/9781137388575.0011

Studies Conference, Universities of Southampton and Winchester, 29–31 July 2013.

Gray, M. (2013) 'Exploring Pupil Perceptions of Jews, Jewish Identity and the Holocaust', *Journal of Modern Jewish Studies*, 12: 3 (Forthcoming).

Gray, M. (2014) 'Preconceptions of the Holocaust among Thirteen and Fourteen Year Olds in English Schools'. Unpublished PhD Thesis, Institute of Education, University of London (Forthcoming).

Greenspan, H. (2010) *On Listening to Holocaust Survivors: Beyond Testimony* (Minnesota: Paragon House).

Gross, M. (2013) 'To Teach the Holocaust in Poland: Understanding Teachers' Motivations to Engage the Painful Past', *Intercultural Education*, 24: 1–2, 103–120.

Gross, Z. and Stevick E. D. (2010) 'Holocaust Education – International Perspectives: Challenges, Opportunities and Research', *Prospects*, 40: 1, 17–33.

Gryglewski, E. (2010) 'Teaching about the Holocaust in Multicultural Societies: Appreciating the Learner', *Intercultural Education*, 21: S1, S41–S49.

Haggith, T. and Newman, J. (2005) 'Introduction', in Haggith, T. and Newman, J. (Eds) *Holocaust and the Moving Image: Representations in Film and Television since 1933* (London: Wallflower Press).

Hajič, J., Ircing, P. and Psutka, J. (2012) 'Searching Their Voices', *Past Forward*, Summer 2012, 28–29.

Hansen, J. (2013) 'Auschwitz Is Made of Lego and Hitler Hates Beckham: YouTube and the Future of Holocaust Remembrance'. Paper presented at *The Future of Holocaust Studies Conference*, Universities of Southampton and Winchester, 29–31 July 2013.

Hargreaves, D. (1996) *Teaching as a Research-Based Profession: Possibilities and Prospects* (London: Teacher Training Agency).

Harris, D. (2005) 'Foreword', in Smith, T. (Ed.) *The Holocaust and Its Implications: A Seven-Nation Comparative Study* (New York: American Jewish Committee).

Harrison, C., Comber, C., Fisher, T., Haw, K., Lunzer, E., McFarlane, A., Mavers, D., Scrimshaw, P., Somekh, B. and Watling, R. (2002) *ImpaCT2: The Impact of Information and Communication Technologies on Pupil Learning and Attainment* (Coventry: Becta).

Hartman, G. (2009) 'Foreword', in Alexander, J. C. (Ed.) *Remembering the Holocaust: A Debate* (Oxford: Oxford University Press).

DOI: 10.1057/9781137388575.0011

Haut Conseil à l'intégration. (2011) *Les défis de l'intégration à l'école.*

Hew, K. F. and Brush, T. (2007) 'Integrating Technology into K–12 Teaching and Learning: Current Knowledge Gaps and Recommendations for Future Research', *Educational Technology Research and Development*, 55: 3, 223–252.

Hintze, M. (2012) 'A Surprising Quantum', *Past Forward*, Summer 2012, 12–13.

Hirsch, M. and Spitzer, L. (2009) 'The Witness in the Archive: Holocaust Studies/Memory Studies', *Memory Studies*, 2: 2, 151–170.

Hondius, D. (2010) 'Finding Common Good in Education about the Holocaust and Slavery', *Intercultural Education*, 21: S1, S61–S69.

Houwink ten Cate, J. (2010) 'The Future of Holocaust Studies', *Jewish Political Studies Review*, 22: 1–2, 33–41.

Isaacs, L., Rosov, W., Raff, L., Rosenblatt, S., Hecht, S., Rozenek, M. and Rotem, Z. (2006) 'Best Practices in Holocaust Education': Report to the San Francisco Jewish Community Endowment Fund, Jewish Education Service of North America.

Ivanova, E. (2004) 'Ukrainian High School Students' Understanding of the Holocaust', *Holocaust and Genocide Studies*, 18: 3, 402–420.

Jaeger, J. (2010) 'Holocaust Resources on the Web', *College and Research Libraries News*, 71: 2, 80–87.

Jedwab, J. (2010) 'Measuring Holocaust Knowledge and Its Impact: A Canadian Case Study', *Prospects*, 40: 2, 273–287.

Jennings, L. (2010) 'Challenges and Possibilities of Holocaust Education and Critical Citizenship: An Ethnographic Study of a Fifth-Grade Bilingual Class Revisited', *Prospects*, 40: 1, 35–56.

Jikeli, G. (2013) 'Perceptions of the Holocaust among Young Muslims in Berlin, Paris and London', in Jikeli, G. and Allouche-Benayoun, J. (Eds) *Perceptions of the Holocaust in Europe and Muslim Communities, Muslims in Global Societies Series* (New York: Springer) 105–131.

Kangisser Cohen, S. (2010) 'Survivors of the Holocaust and Their Children', *Journal of Modern Jewish Studies*, 9: 2, 165–183.

Katz, D. (2009) 'On Three Definitions: Genocide, Holocaust Denial, Holocaust Obfuscation' in Donskis, L. (Ed.) *A Litmus Test Case of Modernity: Examining Modern Sensibilities and the Public Domain in the Baltic States at the Turn of the Century* (Bern: Peter Lang) 259–277.

Kelso, M. (2013) ' "And Roma were Victims Too." The Romani Genocide and Holocaust Education in Romania', *Intercultural Education*, 24, 1–2, 61–78.

DOI: 10.1057/9781137388575.0011

Kinloch, N. (2001) 'Parallel Catastrophes? Uniqueness, Redemption and the Shoah', *Teaching History*, 104, 8–14.

Kushner, T. (2006) 'Holocaust Testimony, Ethics and the Problem of Representation', *Poetics Today*, 27: 2, 275–295.

Lange, A. (2008) *A Survey of Teachers' Experiences and Perceptions in Relation to Teaching about the Holocaust* (Stockholm: Living History Forum).

Laub, D. (2009) 'On Holocaust Testimony and Its "Reception" Within Its Own Frame, as a Process in Its Own Right: *A Response to "Between History and Psychoanalysis" by Thomas Trezise*', *History and Memory*, 21: 1, 127–150.

Lazar, A. and Hirsch, T. (2013) 'An Online Partner for Holocaust Remembrance Education: Students Approaching the Yahoo! Answers Community', *Educational Review*, DOI: 10.1080/00131911.2013.839545.

Lee, P. (2004) ' "Walking Backwards into Tomorrow": Historical Consciousness and Understanding History', *International Journal of Historical Learning, Teaching and Research*, 4: 1, 1–46.

Levine, P. (2013) 'And After They Are Gone?' Paper presented at *The Future of Holocaust Studies Conference*, Universities of Southampton and Winchester, 29–31 July 2013.

Levy, D. and Sznaider, N. (2002) 'Memory Unbound: The Holocaust and the Formation of Cosmopolitan Memory', *European Journal of Social Theory*, 5: 1, 87–106.

Lindenbaum, S. (2012) 'Testimony on Location', *Past Forward*, Summer 2012, 10–11.

London Jewish Cultural Centre (2009) 'Full Scale of Holocaust Unknown to British Children', Press Release.

Lustig, B. (2013) 'When Everything Changed', *Past Forward*, Summer 2012, 6–9.

Macgilchrist, F. and Christophe, B. (2011) 'Translating Globalization Theories into Educational Research: Thoughts on Recent Shifts in Holocaust Education', *Discourse: Studies in the Cultural Politics of Education*, 32: 1, 145–158.

Magen, S. (2012) 'Using Testimony in Holocaust Education', The International School for Holocaust Studies, Yad Vashem.

Magid, S. (2012) 'The Holocaust and Jewish Identity in America: Memory, the Unique, and the Universal', *Jewish Social Studies: History, Culture, Society*, 18: 2, 100–135.

Magilov, D. (2007) 'Counting to Six Million: Collecting Projects and Holocaust Memorialization', *Jewish Social Studies*, 14: 1, 23–39.

Maio, H., Traum, D. and Debevec, P. (2012) 'New Dimensions in Testimony', *Past Forward*, Summer 2012, 22–26.

DOI: 10.1057/9781137388575.0011

Maitles, H., Cowan, P. and Butler, E. (2006) 'Never Again!: Does Holocaust Education Have an Effect on Pupils' Citizenship Values and Attitudes?' Scottish Executive Social Research.

Maitles, H. and Cowan, P. (2008) 'More Open to Diversity?: The Longer Term Citizenship Impact of Learning about the Holocaust', in Reflecting on Identities: Research, Practice and Innovation. Children's Identity and Citizenship in Europe, London, 521–530. ISBN 978–0–9560454–7–8, 525–526.

Martin, K. (2007) 'Teaching the Shoah: Four Approaches that Draw Students in', *The History Teacher*, 40: 4, 493–502.

McIntyre, M. (2008) 'To What Extent and in What Ways Does a Facing History and Ourselves Course on Holocaust and Human Behaviour Impact Students' Knowledge of and Attitudes Towards the Holocaust? MA Education (History and Citizenship), Institute of Education, University of London, Unpublished MA Thesis.

Michaels, D. (2013) 'Holocaust Education in the 'Black Hole of Europe': Slovakia's Identity Politics and History Textbooks Pre- and Post-1989', *Intercultural Education*, 24: 1–2, 19–40.

Misco, T. (2007) 'Holocaust Curriculum Development for Latvian Schools: Arriving at Purposes, Aims, and Goals through Curriculum Deliberation', *Theory and Research in Social Education*, 35: 3, 393–426.

Misco, T. (2008) ' "We Did Also Save People": A Study of Holocaust Education in Romania after Decades of Historical Silence', *Theory and Research in Social Education*, 36: 2, 61–94.

Misco, T. (2011) ' "Most Learn almost Nothing": Building Democratic Citizenship by Engaging Controversial History through Inquiry in Post-Communist Europe' *Education, Citizenship, and Social Justice*, 6: 1, 87–104.

Milerski, B. (2010) 'Holocaust Education in Polish Public Schools: Between Remembrance and Civic Education', *Prospects*, 40: 1, 115–132.

Montreal Holocaust Memorial Centre (2012) *Annual Report 2011–12*.

Morgan, P. (2010) 'How Can We Deepen and Broaden Post-16 Students' Historical Engagement with the Holocaust? Developing a Rationale and Methods for Using Film', *Teaching History*, 141, 27–32.

Morse, D. (1981) Studying the Holocaust and Human Behaviour: Effects on Early Adolescent Self-Esteem, Locus of Control, Acceptance of Self and Others, and Philosophy of Human Nature, Unpublished Dissertation, Boston College.

DOI: 10.1057/9781137388575.0011

Moses, A. D. (2003) 'Genocide and Holocaust Consciousness in Australia', *History Compass*, 1: 1, 1–11.

Murphy, K. (2010) 'Example of Best Practice 1. Teaching a Holocaust Case Study in a Post-Conflict Environment: Education as Part of Violence, Reconstruction and Repair', *Intercultural Education*, 21: S1, S71–S77.

Murray, S. (2008) 'Digital Images, Photo-Sharing, and Our Shifting Notions of Everyday Aesthetics', *Journal of Visual Culture*, 7: 2, 147–163.

Nates, T. (2010) " 'But, Apartheid Was Also Genocide... What about Our Suffering?" Teaching the Holocaust in South Africa – Opportunities and Challenges', *Intercultural Education*, 21: S1, S17–S26.

Next Generations (2013) www.nextgenerations.org

Novick, P. (1999) *The Holocaust in American Life* (New York: Houghton Mifflin Co.).

Office for Democratic Institutions and Human Rights (2005) *Education on the Holocaust and on Anti-Semitism*.

Ostrower, C. (2000) *Humour as a Defence Mechanism in the Holocaust.* Unpublished PhD Thesis, Tel-Aviv University.

Otsuka, M. (1999) 'Importance of Holocaust Education in Japan', *Journal of Genocide Research*, 1: 3, 459–462.

Pearce, A. (2014) *Holocaust Consciousness in Contemporary Britain* (Abingdon: Routledge).

People for the Ethical Treatment of Animals (2013) www.peta.org. Accessed 3 September 2013.

Peterson, T. (2010) 'Moving beyond the Toolbox: Teaching Human Rights through Teaching the Holocaust in Post-Apartheid South Africa', *Intercultural Education*, 21, S1, S27–S31.

Pettigrew, A. Foster, S. Howson, J. Salmons, P. Lenga, R.-A. and Andrews, K. (2009) *Teaching about the Holocaust in English Secondary Schools: An Empirical Study of National Trends, Perspectives and Practice* (Holocaust Education Development Programme, Institute of Education, University of London).

Pfanzelter, E. (2013) 'The Holocaust and Social Networks: Memory, Commemoration or Forums for Anti-Semitism and Racism?' Paper presented at *The Future of Holocaust Studies Conference*, Universities of Southampton and Winchester, 29–31 July 2013.

Polak, K. (2010) 'Tolerance Education in Morocco. "Anne Frank: A History for Today": Learning about Our Past – Contributing to Our Future', *Intercultural Education*, 21: S1, S51–S59.

DOI: 10.1057/9781137388575.0011

Rensmann, L. (2005) *Holocaust Education in Germany: An Interview*. PBS Frontline (19 May 2005).

Richardson, Alasdair. (2012) *Holocaust Education: An Investigation into the Types of Learning that Take Place When Students Encounter the Holocaust*. Unpublished PhD Thesis, Brunel University.

Richardson, Anna. (2005) 'The Ethical Limitations of Holocaust Literacy Representation', *eSharp*, 5 (University of Glasgow).

Rideout, V., Foehr, U. and Roberts, D. (2010) *Generation M2: Media in the Lives of 8- to 18-year Olds* (California: A Kaiser Family Foundation Study).

Riley, K. and Totten, S. (2002) 'Understanding Matters: Holocaust Curricula and the Social Studies Classroom', *Theory and Research in Social Education*, 30: 4, 541–562.

Riley, K., Washington, E. and Humphries, E. (2011) 'Facing History and Ourselves: Noble Purpose, Unending Controversy', in Totten, S. and Pedersen, J. (Eds) *Teaching and Studying Social Issues: Major Programs and Approaches* (Charlotte, North Carolina: Information Age Publishing) 119–139.

Rosenfeld, A. (1995) 'The Americanization of the Holocaust', *Commentary*, 99: 6, 35–41.

Rothberg, M. and Stark, J. (2003) 'After the Witness: A Report from the Twentieth Anniversary Conference of the Fortunoff Video Archive for Holocaust Testimonies at Yale', *History and Memory*, 15: 1, 85–96.

Rothman, M. (2010) 'Building a Tree of Testimony', *Past Forward*, Summer 2010, 17.

Rüsen, J. (1990) *Zeit und Sinn: Strategien jistoischen Denkens* (Frankfurt: Fischer TB).

Rutland, S. (2010) 'Creating Effective Holocaust Education Programmes for Government Schools with Large Muslim Populations in Sydney', *Prospects*, 40: 1, 75–91.

Salmons, P. (2001) 'Moral Dilemmas: History Teaching and the Holocaust', *Teaching History*, 104, 34–40.

Salmons, P. (2010) 'Universal Meaning or Historical Understanding: The Holocaust in History and History in the Curriculum', *Teaching History*, 141, 57–63.

Salmons, P. (2012) *Holocaust Memorial Day: How Secure Is Holocaust Memory?* Huffington Post (27 January 2012).

Santerini, M. (2003) 'Holocaust Education in Italy', *Intercultural Education*, 14: 2, 225–232.

DOI: 10.1057/9781137388575.0011

Schilling, D. (1996) 'The Dead End of Demonizing: Dealing with the Perpetrators in Teaching the Holocaust', in Millen, R. (Ed.) *New Perspectives on the Holocaust: A Guide for Teachers and Scholars* (New York: New York University Press).

Schultz, L., Barr, D. and Selman, R. (2001) 'The Value of a Developmental Approach to Evaluating Character Development Programmes: An Outcome Study of Facing History and Ourselves', *Journal of Moral Education*, 30: 1, 3–27.

Schwartz, D. (1990) '"Who Will Tell Them after We're Gone?": Reflections on Teaching the Holocaust', *The History Teacher*, 23: 2, 95–110.

Schweber, S. (2003) 'Simulating Survival', *Curriculum Inquiry*, 33: 2, 139–188.

Schweber, S. (2006) 'Holocaust Fatigue', *Social Education*, 7: 1, 44–50.

Schweber, S. (2008) '"Here There Is No Why": Holocaust Education at a Lubavitch Girls' Yeshivah', *Jewish Social Studies*, 14: 2, 156–185.

Schweber, S. (2008) '"What Happened to Their Pets?": Third Graders Encounter the Holocaust', *Teachers College Record*, 110: 10, 2073–2115.

Schweber, S. (2010) 'Education', in Hayes, P. and Roth, J. (Eds) *The Oxford Handbook of Holocaust Studies* (Oxford: Oxford University Press) 695–708.

Sepinwall, H. (1999) 'Incorporating Holocaust Education into K–4 Curriculum and Teaching in the United States', *Social Studies and the Young Learner*, 10: 3, 5–8.

Shahabi, C., Khodaei, A. and Fishbain, B. (2012) 'Geo-Immersive Learning', *Past Forward*, Summer 2012, 11–12.

Shemilt, D. (2006) 'The Future of the Past: How Adolescents Make Sense of Past, Present and Future'. Paper presented the International Invitation Conference: *National History Standards: The Problem of the Canon and the Future of History Teaching*, University of Utrecht, October 2006.

Shoham, E. Shiloah, N. and Kalisman, R. (2003) 'Arab Teachers and Holocaust Education: Arab Teachers Study Holocaust Education in Israel', *Teaching and Teacher Education* 19, 609–625.

Short, G. (2003) 'Lessons of the Holocaust: A Response to the Critics', *Educational Review*, 55: 3, 277–287.

Short, G. (2005) 'Learning from Genocide? A Study in the Failure of Holocaust Education', *Intercultural Education*, 16: 4, 367–380.

Short, G. (2013) 'Reluctant Learners? Muslim Youth Confront the Holocaust', *Intercultural Education*, 24: 1–2, 121–132.

DOI: 10.1057/9781137388575.0011

Silverstein, J. (2012) ' "From the Utter Depth of Degradation to the Apogee of Bliss": The Genderings of Diasporic Zionism and Jewish Holocaust Education', *Journal of Modern Jewish Studies*, 11: 3, 377–398.

Smith, T. (1995) *Holocaust Denial: What the Survey Data Reveal* (New York: American Jewish Committee).

Smith, T. (2005) *The Holocaust and Its Implications: A Seven-Nation Comparative Study* (New York: American Jewish Committee).

Smith, S. (2010) 'Online: First Testimonies on the Internet', *Past Forward*, Summer 2010, 3.

Smith, S. (2013) 'Editorial', *Past Forward*, Summer 2013, 6.

Snyder, T. (2010) *Bloodlands: Europe between Hitler and Stalin* (New York: Basic Books).

Solomon, A. (2011) *The Paradox of Holocaust Humour: ComedyTthat Illuminates Tragedy* (New York: Proquest, Umi Dissertation Publishing, City University of New York).

Stevick, D. (2012) 'The Holocaust in the Contemporary Baltic States: International Relations, Politics, and Education, Holocaust', *Study and Research* (Holocaust: Studii şi cercetări), 1: 5, 87–103.

Stevick, D. and Michaels, D. (2013) 'Empirical and Normative Foundations of Holocaust Education: Bringing Research and Advocacy into Dialogue', *Intercultural Education*, 24: 1–2, 1–18.

Street, K. (2013) 'Standing at the Intersection', *Past Forward*, Summer 2013, 16–17.

Strom, M. and Parsons, W. (1984) *Facing History and Ourselves: Holocaust and Human Behaviour* (New York: Facing History and Ourselves National Foundation).

Tartakovsky, D. (2008) 'Conflicting Holocaust Narratives in Moldovan Nationalist Historical Discourse', *East European Jewish Affairs*, 38: 2, 211–229.

Task Force for International Cooperation, Holocaust Education, Remembrance and Research (2010) 'Educational Working Group Paper on the Holocaust and Other Genocides'.

Task Force for International Cooperation, Holocaust Education, Remembrance and Research (2010) 'Educational Working Group Paper on Teaching the Holocaust without Survivors'.

Telegraph (2013) 'Teenagers "Spend an Average of 31 Hours Online" '. http://www.telegraph.co.uk. Accessed 3 October 2013.

Totten, S. (1998) 'The Start Is as Important as the Finish', *Social Education*, 62: 2, 70–76.

DOI: 10.1057/9781137388575.0011

Totten, S. (1999) 'Should There Be Holocaust Education for K–4 Students? The Answer Is No', *Social Sciences and the Young Learner*, 12: 1, 36–39.

Trezise, T. (2008) 'Between History and Psychoanalysis: A Case Study in the Reception of Holocaust Survivor Testimony', *History and Memory*, 20: 1, 7–47.

USC Shoah Foundation. (2013) sfi.usc.edu/

USHMM and Salzburg Global Seminar (2013) *Global Perspectives on Holocaust Education: Trends, Patterns and Practices* (Working Draft) (Washington DC: USHMM).

Van Driel, B. and Van Dijk, L. (2010) 'Diverse Classrooms – Opportunities and Challenges', *Intercultural Education*, 21: S1, S1–S5.

Vice, S. (2011) 'Claude Lanzmann's Einsatzgruppen Interviews', *Holocaust Studies: A Journal of Culture and History*, 17: 2–3, 51–74.

Vice, S. (2013) 'Holocaust Perpetrator in Teaching and Research'. Paper presented at *The Future of Holocaust Studies Conference*, Universities of Southampton and Winchester, 29–31 July 2013.

Von Borries, B. (2003) 'Attitudes of Teachers and Pupils Towards the Shoa in Germany', *Intercultural Education*, 14: 2, 201–214.

Wenglinsky, H. (1998) *Does It Compute? The Relationship between Educational Technology and Student Achievement in Mathematics* (Princeton, NJ: Policy Information Center of the Educational Testing Service).

Welzer, H. (2008) 'Collateral Damage of History Education: National Socialism and the Holocaust in German Family Memory', *Social Research*, 75: 1, 287–314.

Xu, X. (2009) 'Holocaust Education in China', *The Holocaust and the United Nations Outreach Programme Discussion Papers Journal* (New York: United Nations).

Yablonka, H. (2003) 'The Development of Holocaust Consciousness in Israel: The Nuremberg, Kapos, Kastner and Eichmann Trials', *Israel Studies*, 8: 3, 1–24.

Zembrzycki, S. and High, S. (2012) "When I Was Your Age': Bearing Witness in Holocaust Education in Montreal', *The Canadian Historical Review*, 93: 3, 408–435.

Index

Adams and Roscigno, 106
AFH, 26, 43, 47
AJC, 3, 45
Alexander, 61
Americanisation, 75, 76
Andrews, 37, 59, 84, 89, 97
Android, 102
Anne Frank, 26, 35, 47, 75, 104
   diary, 12, 15, 43, 47, 75
antisemitism, 9, 13, 29, 87
Arab–Israeli conflict, 28, 29
Argentina, 26
Auron, 11
Auschwitz, 11, 46, 49,102, 105,
   113
Australia, 30, 62, 87
Austria, 3, 35, 84
Avraham, 24

Buszkowski, 23
Balberg, 69
Banks, Cresswell and Ainley,
   100
Barnouw, 75
Barr, 52
Bartov, 91, 92, 97
Bastel, Mtzka and Miklas, 35
Bauer, 33, 65
Beaver, 86, 96
Bhana, 35
Bialystok, 73, 75
Bischoping, 45
Blutinger, 36, 90, 94, 97, 98
Bosnia-Herzegovina, 47
Broadcastr, 102, 110

Browning, 85, 91, 92, 93, 98
Bulgaria, 83
Burundi, 62
Byford, 92

Caldwell, 62
Cambodia, 27
Cameroon, 62
Canada, 3, 15, 83
Carr, 30
Cassutto, 107
Centre for Holocaust
   Education, 54, 89
Chile, 26
China, 28
Chyrikins and Vieyra, 26
Clark, 86
Clements, 90
Clyde, 35
Cohen, 6, 83
Cole, 69
collecting projects, 63
Columbia, 54
conscience design, 108
cosmopolitan memory, 61
Cowan and Maitles, 35
curriculum, 4
Czech Republic, 102, 110

Dachau, 45
Daniel, 100
Darnell, 104, 106, 113
defiance, 55
Democratic Republic of
   Congo, 62

130   *Index*

De Vaus, 45
Doneson, 65
Donovan and Bransford, 2
Downfall, 105
Dreier, 84

Ecker, 87
Eckmann, 47, 71, 72
Edwards and ODowd, 11
Egypt, 30
Einsatzgruppen, 12
Elie Wiesel, 82
Ene, 16
England. *See* UK
Epstein, 36
Estonia, 23

Facebook, 104, 107
Fallace, 56, 73
Fanning, 107
FHAO, 15, 16, 27
Fine, 52
First World War, 88
Fortunoff Video Archive, 84
Foster, 4, 96
France, 3
Frankl, 10
Friedländer, 91
Fuchs and Woessmann, 100

Geo-Immersion, 109, 110
Germany, 3, 10, 11, 24, 30, 68
Gerstenfeld, 74, 80
globalisation, 69, 76
Google Trends, 106
Gray, 12, 15, 19, 20, 37, 55, 59, 66
Greece, 16
Greenman, 89
Greenspan, 92
Gross, 6
Gross and Stevick, 22
Gryglewski, 24
Guatemala, 26

Haggith and Newman, 65
Hajiè, Ircing and Psutka, 102
Hargreaves, 53, 54

Harrison et al., 100
HEDP, 3, 83
Herscovitch, 85, 86, 87, 96, 97
HET, 83
Hew and Brush, 100
Hintze, 102
Hirsch and Spitzer, 61
historical consciousness, 2
Holocaust Denial, 22, 104, 106, 107
Holocaust Fatigue, 37
Holocaust Humour, 64
Holocaust Memorial Day, 12
Hondius, 36
Houwink ten Cate, 54
Hungary, 110

IHRA, 26, 82
Indonesia, 47
iPhone, 102
Israel, 6, 7, 11, 62, 83, 87
Italy, 10, 19, 37, 67
ITF, 26
Ivanova, 8
IWitness, 85, 96, 103

Janusz Korczak, 11
Japan, 28, 67
Jedwab, 3, 4, 17
Jennings, 34
JESNA, 6, 86, 110
Jikeli, 31
Judenräte, 11

Kangisser Cohen, 87
Katz, 22
Kelso, 13
Kennedy, 66
Kindertransport, 35
Kinloch, 47
Kristallnacht, 4

Lange, 3, 4, 5, 15, 29, 45, 54, 70
Lanzmann, 93
Latin America, 26, 28, 44, 51
Latvia, 6, 23
Laub, 91
Lazar and Hirsch, 108

Levine, 94
Levy and Sznaider, 61
Life Is Beautiful, 67
Lindenbaum, 102
London Jewish Cultural Centre, 46
Lustig, 111
Luxembourg, 83

Macgilchrist and Christophe, 76
Madagascar, 62
Magen, 84, 95
Magid, 76
Magilov, 63
Maio, Traum and Debevec, 82, 108
Maitles and Cowan, 13, 14
Majdanek, 35
Majo, Traum and Debevec, 109
March of Remembrance and Hope, 35
Martin, 87, 88
Mauthausen, 35
Maws, 37
McIntyre, 67
Mémorial de la Shoah, 62
Mexico, 67
Michaels, 9
Middle East, 29
Milerski, 24
Misco, 6
Moldova, 23
Molotov-Ribbentrop Pact, 11
Montreal Holocaust Memorial Centre, 83, 85
Morgan, 68
Morocco, 5, 53
Moses, 62
Murphy, 52

Nakba, 29, 30
Nates, 5, 26, 27, 43, 44, 73
Natural Language Understanding, 108
new dimensions in testimony, 108, 109, 113
New Zealand, 62
next generations, 86
Nicaragua, 26

ODIHR, 5, 29, 76, 83

Ostrower, 64

Pearce, 61
perpetrator testimony, 92, 93, 94
Peterson, 27, 39, 47
Pfanzelter, 104, 105, 106
Polak, 5, 85, 96, 97
Poland, 3, 6, 9, 110
Primo Levi, 82

racism, 13, 72
Rensmann, 68
Richardson, Alastair, 33, 36, 64, 90
Richardson, Anna, 65, 90
Riley, Washington and Humphries, 16, 25, 52, 66
Roma, 14, 72
Romania, 6, 9, 14, 23, 83
Rothberg and Stark, 84
Rüsen, 2
Rutland, 30, 31
Rwanda, 27, 72

Salmons, 63, 65, 73, 80
Salzburg Global Seminar, 25
Santerini, 10, 19, 67
Schilling, 94
Schindlers List, 55, 65, 66, 67, 83
Schondorf, 90
Schweber, 8, 15, 18, 41
second generation survivors, 86
Senegal, 62
Shahabi, Khodaei and Fishbain, 109, 110
Shemilt, 2
Shoham, Shiloah and Kalisman, 29, 52
Short, 12
Silverstein, 32, 40
Slovakia, 9
smartphone, 102, 103, 109
Snyder, 22
Solomon, 64
Sophie's Choice, 75
South Africa, 5, 27, 28, 43
South African Holocaust and Genocide Foundation, 26
Spielberg, 85

DOI: 10.1057/9781137388575.0012

SS, 11
Star of David, 11
Stevick, 22
Stevick and Michaels, 68
survivor-speakers, 87
Sweden, 3, 5, 29

Tartakovsky, 23
textbooks, 9
The Boy in the Striped Pyjamas, 12, 46,
    55, 66, 67, 78
The Pianist, 55, 67
Togo, 62
Totten, 8, 18, 20, 33, 34, 38, 40, 50, 59, 78
training, 6, 110, 111
trauma, 33
Treblinka, 45, 94
Trezise, 91
Turkey, 47
Twitter, 103, 104, 107

UK, 3, 5, 11, 15, 29, 30, 31, 32, 35, 36, 46,
    83, 100
Ukraine, 8, 9, 13, 110

USA, 3, 8, 34, 61, 62, 65, 66,
    86, 101
USC Institute for Creative
    Technologies, 108
USC Shoah Foundation Institute
    for Visual History and Education,
    85, 107
USHMM, 7, 103

Van Driel and Van Dijk, 37
vice, 93, 94

Wannsee Conference, 11
Welzer, 10
Wenglinsky, 100

Xu, 28

Yablonka, 62
Yad Vashem, 7, 104
YouTube, 105, 106, 107

Zembrzycki and High, 87, 90, 97
Zoltak, 90
Zytomirski, 104

DOI: 10.1057/9781137388575.0012